"After 35 years of racing in triathlons, working with many different coaches and attending many swim clinics, I have heard the same advice over and over and was never able to transform the teachings into results. After a few swim sessions, Sheila shared great information with me that I had never heard before. I want to thank Sheila for her instruction and the confidence that has resulted from implementing her technique into my stroke. I now have several races under my belt using the technique, and I am happy to report that I always EXPECT to be the first out of the water." ~ *Greyson Quarles, US team member - World Triathlon Age-Group Championships, and Kona Ironman triathlete*

"In my mind, Sheila Taormina may be the greatest athlete in the modern Olympic era. She's the only person that I know who has made four Olympic teams in 3 different sports. Sheila qualified to swim on the 800 freestyle relay where she won a gold medal swimming for the United States. Then four years later she competed in the Olympic triathlon and then four years after that (her third Olympiad), she's on the U. S. Olympic triathlon team again. She then decided she wanted to compete in the modern pentathlon and made the Olympic team and competed once again. Four Olympiads in 3 different sports. I know of no one who has done that in the modern era and possibly ever." ~ *Jim Richardson, Head Coach University of Michigan Women's Swim Team*

CALL the SUIT

**Develop the Freestyle Swim Technique
Used by the Fastest Swimmers in the World**

Sheila Taormina

Triathlon World Champion, Olympic Swimming Gold Medalist

Cover photo of Peter Vanderkaay, 2008 Olympic gold medalist,
by Daniel J. Smith, DanielJS111@aol.com
http://djsmithphotography.blogspot.com

Back cover author photo by Gale Bernhardt

All photographs, unless otherwise noted,
by Daniel J. Smith, DanielJS111@aol.com
http://djsmithphotography.blogspot.com

Mike Troy and Mark Spitz photos permission
to reprint from Indiana University,
The Counsilman Center for the Science of Swimming

Johnny Weissmuller photos permission to reprint from
International Swimming Hall of Fame

The Halo Swim Training System™ is a trademark
of Lane Gainer Company

Dandilines.com
11426 Centennial
Whitmore Lake, Mi 48189
donna@dandilines.com

The information in this book is true and complete to the best of our
knowledge. All recommendations are made without any guarantee on the
part of the Author or Publisher, who also disclaim any liability incurred
in connection with the use of this data or specific details.

Library of Congress Cataloging-in-Publication Data Available

First paperback edition 2010

ISBN 978-0-9828160-0-4

Printed in the United States of America by
Thomson-Shore, Inc., Dexter, Michigan

10 9 8 7 6 5 4 3 2 1

CALL the SUIT

**Develop the Freestyle Swim Technique
Used by the Fastest Swimmers in the World**

Sheila Taormina

Triathlon World Champion, Olympic Swimming Gold Medalist

dandilines.com

Dedicated to Greg Phill, my swim coach. You lifted the cement blocks off my shoulders before the Olympic Trials, the moment you quoted John Lubbock,

"When we have done our best, we should wait the result in peace."

. . . Also thank you for reminding me that a couple billion people never knew when I had a bad race.

Contents

Call the Suit in Live Action

Below you will find a QR Code that has been placed to create a completely interactive book.

A QR Code is a two-dimensional barcode that when scanned by a mobile phone with the appropriate Barcode application will transport the user from the physical world to the virtual world via hardlink or hyperlink.

To take advantage of this technology, download a Barcode/QR Code scanner application (many free options available online) on your smartphone or your computer with optical capabilities. Open the application and scan the barcode below. You will be sent to a video that shows the techniques described in this book.

We hope you find it to be a valuable tool. If you do not have scanning capabilities on your phone or computer, then please visit www.sheilat.com to view the videos.

Video 1

Video 2

Video 3

Acknowledgments

First, to my mom and dad.

Mom, for your prayers above all else - but also - for a woman who says she was made of bubble gum and rubber bands, and who I never saw get her hair wet at a pool, and who, if I asked you today to tell me what you thought was my best 200 Freestyle time you would say something like three minutes because you have no clue about times - for all that, you made the perfect swimming mom. And dad, for your ability, after 87 years on this earth, to sum up your life in four words, and for the great swim lessons, you are my hero.

To my twin brother, Steven, for copy-editing this book, and for keeping Doc Counsilman's camp booklet with the revealing underwater photos that I stared at for hours before 1996. Growing up with you as a number one friend and playmate is a treasure worth more than all the gold in the world.

To every sister and brother, niece and nephew, and brother/sister in-law, thank you for coming to all four Olympics and cheering just as wildly for a 23rd place finish as a gold medal finish. You know about the true spirit of human endeavor. You are what I love most about life.

To my swim coach Greg Phill, to whom this book is dedicated. If you are taken out of the timeline of my life, then the sports story begins and ends completely differently. And to your amazing wife, Jules - my friend in "the Truth."

To my college coaches, Jack Bauerle and Harvey Humphries at The University of Georgia. There will never be a more perfect duo. I've watched with admiration as you have built the Georgia program to #1 in the country, and I know the foundation upon which it lies. It is authentic, balanced, and as much about life as it is swimming. I am so thankful for all of your guidance and love.

To Coach Jack Nelson, Fort Lauderdale Swim Team. Coach, you have the most beautiful, believing mind. I am thankful that even a sliver of that belief seeped into my mind, because technique alone does not win a race. You will go down in history as a coach who took the impossible and made it possible because of belief- the 1976 Women's 4 x 100 Freestyle Relay team that brought home gold against GDR. You are a rock star, and so is every girl on that team!

To Jim Richardson, head women's swim coach at The University of Michigan, thank you for making available, on a daily basis, U of M's 50 meter pool before 1996. The encouragement you gave Greg and me during those days was a true gift, and your dry erase board lessons on swimming technique opened new levels of understanding for me.

To Greyson and Georgie Quarles, for your genuine friendship, and for welcoming my cats and me to your house in the warm Florida Keys during the winter of 2010 so that I could write this book. Thank you for sharing your blessings. P.S.- The cats want to go back....no pressure - I'm just relaying the message.

To Matt Farrell at United States Swimming, for tracking down historical information and Olympic swimming footage for my personal research. The timeliness in which you responded to my request was exceptional and so very much appreciated.

To Craig Askins from Lane Gainer, not only for supporting my swimming, triathlon and modern pentathlon careers, but also for your help on the technical aspects of taking underwater photos for this book.

To Dave Tanner and Joel Stager who are carrying the torch forward to preserve, and build upon, the work of Doc Counsilman, the greatest pioneer in the history of swimming. You two, in that cubby-hole office on Indiana University's campus have a hidden jewel. It was an honor to meet you and see all of Doc's old cameras and equipment. Also, thank you for granting permission to reprint Doc's original photos of Mike Troy and Mark Spitz.

To Stan Gerbig, photographer at Indiana University, for giving an entire day to take early test rounds of underwater photos. Your generosity helped get this book off the ground.

To my brother-in-law David for taking the very first underwater test pictures at Eastern Michigan University, with last minute notice....so very much appreciated! And to Peter Linn, Head swim coach at Eastern Michigan University for arranging the pool availability for those photos.

To Jeff Kempf, Pool Supervisor at Whitmore Lake High School, for opening the pool and giving countless hours of your time while the final photos for the book were captured. And to Denise Kerrigan, Whitmore Lake Community Recreation and Athletic Director, for your support of the project, in granting permission to use the pool. Thank you so much.

To Donna Shubel - publisher, designer, inventor, photographer, and friend extraordinaire! Your talents are woven throughout this entire book. If I am blessed enough to look at these pages 50 years from now, I will see your hand print on every page. Thank you from the place where Thanks are most deep.

To Mike Shubel and Thomson-Shore Printing for the highest levels of professionalism, quality and service throughout this process. If I had Eli Goldratt's phone number, I would call and let him know that you are doing him proud.

To Rolf Zettersten, for editing this book, but beyond that for your guidance into the world of publishing and writing. Your encouragement gave me the confidence to see this through. Thank you.

To Bruce Wigo, Executive Director at The International Swimming Hall Of Fame in Fort Lauderdale, for your wonderful support in tracking down historical information and for granting permission to use Johnny Weissmuller's photo. Thank you for all you do to preserve swimming history.

To Daniel Smith, for the exceptional final photos you captured for this book. Simply put, you are a champion of life. Thank you for making time in your busy schedule, driving back and forth to Michigan, to work on this project. Your creativity and work ethic are far beyond what I could have hoped for, or asked from you.

To Jim Cahill for your gracious spirit to be the subject of "the low elbow." When the guys give you grief for that, just show them your marathon time. Mostly, thank you for your wonderful friendship.

A special thanks to Price Fishback, my Economics Professor at The University of Georgia. Price, thank you for making a potentially dry subject incredibly applicable to life.

Also, to my production management and business professors at The University of Georgia - Jim Cox, Gerald Horton, and James Gilbert - for your gifted teaching and genuine interest in my swimming career.

To Elizabeth Haverkate for brewing up countless lattes, mochas, and espressos ...they were fantastic!

To Peter Vanderkaay, Allison Schmitt and Margaret Kelley, for taking the time from your busy schedules to come to the pool for the photos. You represent the sport of swimming beautifully. I wish you all great success as you carry the torch towards 2012. And to Allison's parents, Ralph and Gail Schmitt - thank you for giving up your daughter for a half day during her short visit home.

To Eric Baumgartner, Assistant Athletic Director at The University of Georgia for providing the NCAA compliance information in such a timely manner.

Above all, a thank you to God, for blessing my life with health, opportunity, and the people who are mentioned in this book and many others.

Introduction

How is it that the elite swimmers in the world have just spun through the 2008 Olympics in Beijing and 2009 World Championships in Rome, tearing apart almost every world record, while masses of triathletes, masters swimmers, and age-groupers are stumped as to why their times are barely improving, or not improving at all?

The elite swimming times are almost unreal. One would think that at some point it has to stop. Consider for a moment that the women's world records are now as fast as the men's world records from the early 1970s. That means that even Mark Spitz's times from the 1972 Games are being met by the fastest women today. The 200 Meter Freestyle is a perfect example. Today's world record for women is 1:52.98. Spitz won Olympic gold in Munich in 1:52.78.

It doesn't matter which stroke you choose, nor which distance. In the 50 Meter Freestyle, South African Jonty Skinner held the world record in 1976 with a time of 23.86. On August 2, 2009 Britta Steffen of Germany powered to a 23.73.

Today's 1500 Meter Freestyle world record for women, 15:42.54, is 10 seconds faster than the gold medal, world record setting time for men at the 1972 Olympics, 15:52.58.

The elite male swimmers are doing the same thing the women are doing - smashing previous marks at a rate that has left most people scratching their heads. It makes the statement made by the famous Johnny Weissmuller almost comical. Weissmuller, who won 5 Olympic gold medals in swimming at the 1924 and 1928 Games, stated in his book, *Swimming The American Crawl* (published in 1930) in the chapter, "Can The Crawl Be Improved?":

"My technique has been called the 'perfected' crawl stroke because it reduced water resistance to the minimum; it facilitated a method of breathing that most closely approximates the natural, involuntary method of nature; it put the body in a position to make free and unimpeded use of all its strength and power and leverage, and it got the most propulsion for the effort expended. Some say there is still room for improvement in this stroke. I do not see just where the improvement will come." [1]

Now, we have to give Weissmuller some slack for thinking the world would never improve upon what he did in the roaring '20s, because he did set 67 world records during his swimming career. He was never beaten in an official swimming race. Think about it - NEVER beaten! If I was him then I probably would have thought I had perfected the "crawl" too. Also, it wasn't like he just dove in and swam any old way he wanted. In his book he describes, down to the smallest details, the reasons why he used the technique he used. A great deal of thought went into it.

What was that technique? You may know it as the Tarzan drill - the drill you do in practice where you hold your head above the water. If your coach is a fun person, then he or she will insist you do the ululating Tarzan yell while you stroke; mine did.

That was Weissmuller's stroke - to keep his chest and shoulders high in the water, and the drill is called the Tarzan drill because Weissmuller became even more famous after his swimming career when he landed the role of Tarzan in the movies. Below is another excerpt from his book in which he describes his stroke:

"I swim with my chest and shoulders high in the water. This enables me to hydroplane, like a speedboat, reducing resistance to a minimum. I swim higher in the water than anybody ever did before, higher than anybody else does to this day…. The height of my chest enables me to arch my back, avoiding the strain of the swayback position which many have to take in order to get the face out of the water for inhaling. The high chest and shoulders and the arch of the back throw my feet lower in the water, where they maintain traction at all times." [2]

Continuing on, Weissmuller wrote that he also believed the hips should stay flat, because, as he explains, if the hips roll then the corresponding arm and shoulder dip lower in the water, thus causing resistance.

Today, we know of course, that freestyle swim technique is the exact opposite. The only people holding their heads above water are people who do not want to get their hair wet, like my mom, and it is most certainly on everyone's radar that hip roll is a common denominator among great swimming champions.

So, are you wondering where I'm going with this?

I am going somewhere very specific, and if you think we are headed for a discussion on reducing resistance, then you have to guess again. Rather, I am going to use Weissmuller and a number of other swimmers who have reigned in the pool for the past five decades to present a picture of swimming that is long overdue - a picture that answers a great many questions.

To begin painting this picture I have to set the scene with the following statement. It may shock you:

Even though Weissmuller's times have long been shattered (his 100 Free world record was first broken in 1934), his fastest 100 Meter Freestyle still beats 95% of triathletes (even the top professionals), 95% of masters swimmers, and 95% of age-group swimmers today.

It is indeed strange commentary to say that Johnny would beat just about every person reading this book.

Let's look at his times: In February, 1924 Johnny Weissmuller swam a 57.4 in the 100 Meter Freestyle (Long Course Meters). Sure, the world record now is 46.91, set by Cesar Cielo of Brazil (2009 World Championships), and the women's world record is 52.07 (Britta Steffen, Germany, 2009 World Championships), but how many of you who are reading this book would think you're the cat's meow for going a time like Weissmuller's?

And it wasn't just the short races in which Weissmuller set world records. He also owned the 400 and 800 Meter Freestyle records: 4:57.0 in the 400, set in 1923, and 10:22.2 in the 800, set in 1927. Although not nearly as impressive as his 100 Meter Freestyle time, those distance event times would still, even today, place him in the lead, or very near the lead, at any triathlon event going into T-1 ("Transition 1," which is triathlon talk for the change-over from the swim to the bike).

I realize that Weissmuller's times may not impress all of you in the swimming world today, especially his 400 and 800 times (Weissmuller was definitely more of a sprinter than a distance swimmer), which means at this point some of you may think this book is too elementary. It may appear that I am going to address only the crowd that needs to catch up with swimming times that were posted almost 100 years ago. Don't close the book so fast. Even if you are a swimmer with national times, or the coach of a swimmer with those times, this book is perhaps even more intended for you, because it is as much about thought processes as it is about swim technique. You may be on the verge of cracking into the very top of the elite ranks but wonder how you are going to climb the next rung of the ladder. The insights provided in this book will help you do that.

The reason many of us have been stumped about how to make improvements in our times, or how to reach the next level, is not for lack of information but rather for lack of organization of the information. Some swimmers try to work on everything, which means they are working on nothing at all. Other swimmers are working on things that have minimal to zero impact on their times, because they were never truthfully told what is most important and which things must be first developed. This book will change that.

You should know why you do what you do at every moment when you are working on technique or training. This is completely possible, yet it is the one thing I see missing in the resources available to date. Textbooks on the market provide us with massive amounts of information - down to the most minute details of stroke technique - but no one has organized the information in a fashion that guides us toward a focus and thus an effective plan.

The title of the book, *Call The Suit*, comes from a mantra of mine in life and sport relating to "taking charge." In my favorite card game, Euchre, each player is given the opportunity to call the trump (most powerful) suit at various times during the game. The player must look at the hand he/she was dealt and then make a decision on whether to take charge of the play of the game or pass the opportunity to the next player, their competitor. I always encourage people to "Call the suit!" Be bold. Understand what you have in your hand, and then make an informed decision on how to best play the game from there.

Too seldom are we coached on how to do this in relation to most parts of our life. My goal is to show the thought process that will develop this in your swimming, and it will actually be a launching pad for you to apply to other areas of your life as well.

I've limited the following pages to the discussion of one stroke, freestyle, for two reasons. First, I wanted to write a book for triathletes more than any other group. I feel that this group has latched on to one swim technique theory for too long. They have been given only small parts of what they need to know about swimming, and led to believe it is what "swimmers" do. I want to show triathletes the real picture of what "swimmers" do.

The second reason for focusing only on freestyle is simply because it is the stroke that I know inside and out. It is the stroke that took me to the Olympics four times.

I studied it. I spent endless moments thinking about it in the pool, and I got to know it. I am a fraction of an inch over 5'2" on the height scale, so my wingspan was not what put me on the Olympic team - it was the understanding of how to take information and make it work.

If you are new to swimming, please do not be intimidated by this book. The principles are simple. You will understand everything, and you will see exactly the path to your goals.

Lastly, and perhaps most importantly, let's keep everything in perspective - we are not solving any world crisis here. Let's have fun. I am almost certain that if I had to give up coffee in order to do sports, then I probably would have given up the sports (ok, I'm joking…maybe). Either way, make sure to read the dedication if you need some additional perspective, and let's move forward with answering the question from the beginning of the introduction.

Here's wishing you joy on your journey to understanding the beautiful sport of swimming.

Cheers,
Sheila Taormina

Chapter 1

The Pareto Principle
organizing information

Swimming is an incredibly dynamic sport. Every part of our body is doing something all of the time when we swim competitively. The one exception might be the head, which stays neutral and steady at times, but we even need to know what to do with that for the breath. It is an information management nightmare often times, not only for beginners who are trying to learn the sport, but also for experienced swimmers who are at a loss to identify exactly what it is they are missing that will take them to the next level.

In case you have never thought about the complexity of the task, let's contrast swimming with other sports - less dynamic sports in terms of technique. The examples below are two disciplines with which I am familiar, having experienced both on the Olympic stage:

Pistol Shooting - there are great challenges in this sport (remaining focused and calm under pressure), but the technique is very static. A pistol shooter methodically progresses through each step in his/her process, focusing on one element of the sequence at a time, until the shot is fired. Therefore, training shooting technique is not overwhelming. Remaining composed under competition pressure? That is a completely different story, for another book.

Cycling - this sport falls in the middle of the static-dynamic spectrum. While the legs are dynamically powering the pedal stroke, the upper body is quite still. Anytime a cyclist chooses to focus on technique, a smoother pedal stroke for example, he/she needs only to focus on the lower half of the body. Therefore, the learning curve and technique applications are quite manageable. Once again, this sport presents a completely different set of keys to success that make it equally as difficult to succeed as any other sport, but mentally managing technique is not one of them.

Managing technique in swimming, in comparison to these other sports, is a beast of a task. During any given length of the pool a swimmer may choose to perfect one of many elements of the stroke. While working on that one element, the swimmer must also consider how to make it work synchronously with the other parts of the stroke. Then, throw in the fact that this is managed within a medium that is not natural - water - and the recipe is overwhelming. My guess is that, because of all this, a high percentage of people who are reading this book are people who are frustrated as to why their swimming times have not improved after all the hours in the pool. I hear you. I am your biggest cheerleader, believe me. I went through the same frustrations with fencing when learning that for the pentathlon.

Fencing, like swimming, is incredibly dynamic. Every body part is doing something all the time, even down to the fingers that hold the grip, and the timing of every body part is crucial. Although contested in a natural environment for the athlete - land - the true complexity of the sport rears its head in that there is another human being on the other side of the competition strip thwarting every attempted move. During the few years I tried to grasp each detail of fencing technique, from age 36-39, my coaches continually yelled, in their Eastern European accents, "Why you do that!?!" If I was thinking about my arm, then my legs were messing up; if I was thinking about my footwork, then I missed the timing. Then one coach would tell me to lean forward more, and another coach would say to stand up more. There was so much to think about simultaneously that I didn't know where to start, nor did I know which coach to believe.

So, I empathize with anyone learning the sport of swimming and those who have been at it for a while but see no improvements in performance. I also relate to the huge population of coaches and swimmers who have experienced a fair amount of success in swimming but who want to know what it takes to reach the next level, or perhaps even to crack the elite ranks one day.

The good news is, while I cannot help you with your fencing, I can definitely help with your swimming. What we have to do is begin sorting and organizing the information.

The Pareto Principle

The best way I know for sorting information is to employ the Pareto Principle, also known as the 80/20 Rule. The Pareto Principle is not a hard-fast rule; rather, it is applied as a rule of thumb, most commonly in arenas such as business and science. When I first learned about it I saw immediately how it could be a tool for sport. I applied it to my swimming

before the 1996 Olympics and every sport I have done since.

Vilfredo Pareto was an Italian economist who, in the early 1900s, took note that approximately 80% of the wealth in his country belonged to 20% of the people. After his notation, others realized that you could apply this 80/20 concept to many aspects of life. In business, a sales person might note that 80% of sales come from 20% of clients, or even that 80% of problems come from a certain 20% of clients. In our personal lives, we may note that we spend 80% of our time with 20% of our acquaintances, and so on.

The Pareto Principle is essentially **the Law of the Vital Few**. It says that there are a few aspects to anything we do that have the greatest impact. The other 80% of things, added together, do not have near the impact as those vital few.

In sport, if we can identify the vital few things that give the greatest impact, then we are much better equipped to design an effective plan that will bring us closer to our goal. *We do not ignore the other 80% of things that give us some return; we simply know where they fall in the list of prioritizing.*

The 80/20 Rule applied to swimming technique

Since swimming is so dynamic, the only way to get a grip on where to start is to manage the information. The Pareto Principle is a perfect tool for this. In this book I am going to show you the vital few. They are extremely important. They give us 80% of what we need to be a swimmer. Every other detail in our technique does not impact our swimming results nearly as much as the vital

Vilfredo Pareto, Italian industrialist, economist, and philosopher.

Your most important job at swim practice

When you are swimming up and down the pool, you are usually alone with your own thoughts, right? That is when you are hopefully working on your swim technique instead of being off in La-la land. Coaches stand over your lane every once in a while, but for the most part you are in charge of whether you are thinking about technique or "what's for dinner."

I have to drive home the point that technique is, by far, the most important aspect of swimming. Now that I think about it, there is no reason why we cannot apply the 80/20 Rule here. I am going to make the bold claim that technique is 80% of swimming when lined up next to strength, conditioning, or the size of a swimmer.

few. Another way to look at it is that the other details give us minimal benefit unless we have mastered the vital few.

I will still address a few other aspects of swim technique, but this book is focused more on helping you develop the big whoppers. Believe it or not, most people are not working on those. Instead I see them working on the 80% of things that give little return or that give no return without the foundation of the vital few.

There is no top-secret training manual that gold medalists have. The best swimmers in the world do the vital few elements really well, and they think about them most of the time. I might even dare to say they think about them 80% of the time during practice, warm-up included.

Conditioning and strength are very important in swimming, but they will not get us far without good technique. Ask the strongest football player you know to swim one length of the pool. If he has not learned technique, then he will look like a drowning rat in the water, and it is not because his muscles are weighing him down. It is the same with conditioning. You could ask a sub 2:40 marathoner to swim, and if he/she does not know swim technique, then all the conditioning in the world will not help. This is one of the scenarios in which the vital element is important due to the fact that it is the foundation upon which the other elements rely. Technique takes the 80% prize, because without it strength and conditioning mean nothing. That being said, once we have a solid technique developed, then the ratios change, and our physical training kicks in much more.

The reason this has to be stressed is because I see too many athletes allowing their strokes to fall apart when they tire at practice (age-group swimmers mainly). Or, worse off, I see people choosing to forgo technique altogether in order to keep up with their lane mates (triathletes and masters swimmers mainly). The only way you will benefit from reading this book is if you commit to making the vital elements of swim technique a priority.

In fact, my goal is to get you so excited about your understanding of swimming after reading this book that you actually become addicted to making that your focus during practice. Then, once you're on a good roll with technique, the training, conditioning, and strength become fascinating and much more meaningful to apply.

Here we go...

You are probably getting antsy by now to find out which are the vital few elements, or maybe you already skipped ahead to find them. Don't do that just yet. We have to go over the big picture understanding of swimming first. After that we will begin to name the vital few and explain how to develop them. Remember the 80/20 Rule though. I will refer to it later.

So, in honor of Vilfredo, brew up a good Italian roast espresso, take a comfortable seat, and enjoy the next few chapters.

Summary for Chapter 1

1. The Pareto Principle, also known as the 80/20 Rule, is the Law of the Vital Few. We will get our greatest impact (approximately 80%) from only a few (approximately 20%) of the things we do.

2. In swimming, technique is the one aspect that takes us 80% of the way to being a great swimmer. Conditioning and strength do not help us as swimmers if we first do not have good technique.

3. The Pareto Principle is also a helpful tool for knowing which elements of the swim stroke are most important.

4. At swim practice, a person should maintain focus on technique instead of getting sloppy when they are tired or forgoing technique all together in order to keep up with the people in their lane.

Chapter 2

The Big Picture
understanding the swimming equation

Are you ready? Don't be surprised when you see how simple this is. In this chapter you are going to see, perhaps for the first time, the big picture view of swimming. Once you see it, every detail of technique will begin to make sense. You will start to answer questions for yourself, and your swimming will go to a whole new level. You will have confidence, and the laps up and down the pool will begin to mean something. The best part is that it is so simple.

First, let's set the stage *(see fig. 2.1)*: You are going to push off the wall and swim 25 yards. We will assume that you do a nice streamline (please do a nice streamline...thank you). Now you are on the surface swimming.

<u>Only two things</u> affect the time it takes you to get from your breakout to the end of the pool:

1) The number of strokes you take to get across the pool.

2) The rate at which you take those strokes (turnover).

Please note that one stroke is a FULL arm cycle. In other words, one stroke is from when your right arm enters the water until when your right arm goes in again (or left arm to the left arm again). Another way to count strokes is to count "one" when the right arm goes in and then "two" when the left arm goes in, and so on. Both methods of counting are equally acceptable, but in order to be on the same page we are going to count full cycles.

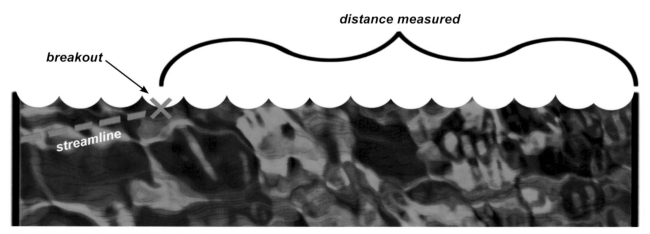

Fig. 2.1 - Side view of a 25 yard pool

Now, let's say that it takes you 10 strokes (full arm cycles) to get to the end of the pool. Let's also say it takes you 1 second per stroke.

If you multiply the number of strokes by the rate at which you take those strokes, then you get your Time. Here is what it looks like in equation form:

(Number of Strokes) x (Rate) = Time
We are going to measure TIME in seconds

Let's insert the numbers from our example:

$$\underset{\text{number of strokes}}{(10 \text{ strokes})} \times \underset{\text{rate}}{(1 \text{ second /stroke})} = \underset{\text{time}}{10 \text{ seconds}}$$

Mathematically it looks like this (remember from math class, we cross out the "strokes" in our equation):

$$10 \ \cancel{\text{strokes}} \ \times \ \frac{1 \text{ second}}{\cancel{\text{stroke}}} = 10 \text{ seconds}$$

That's it. There is the big picture. You can only get faster in swimming in one of two ways:

1) Reduce the number of strokes you take

2) Turnover more quickly

You just learned what I learned at age 25. I had competed in two Olympic Trials (1988 and 1992) before I learned this simple equation. It opened a new level of understanding for me, and I truly believe it helped me make my first Olympic team in 1996. You could take this one thing and run with it. But, of course, there is more to discuss....

While it is true that only two factors affect our swimming time, there are many things that affect those two factors. But, we are on our way. We now have the big picture around which we can frame the details of technique. So, when you read something about swim technique, or if your coach tells you to change your stroke, you should ask yourself how it will influence either the number of strokes you take or the rate at which you take them.

By the way, these two factors are NOT the "vital few" elements from our Pareto Principle discussion. We will get to those soon. What we have just gone over is only the equation that frames the big picture.

Don't Run Off To The Pool Just Yet

Let's look at the equation more closely and take note of how the two factors work in a real life situation.

Since we want to reduce our time in swimming that means that the two factors must be lowered. We can either lower one or the other, or both. The tricky part is that sometimes we get excited that we reduced one, but we forget to check how the other was affected.

The two factors are not always independent of each other. Sometimes the steps we take to reduce one factor end up increasing the other. The best way to explain this is to give two examples.

Example 1: The scenario for this first example goes something like this:

A weekend swimming clinic is advertised as coming to town. It is marketed as the key to unleashing your swimming potential. At the clinic swimmers are told that taking fewer strokes is better. The focus is entirely on reducing the number of strokes to get across the pool. From our equation, we know this is a good thing. BUT, at this clinic, the swimmers were never told about the other half of the equation.

Every participant is in the water all weekend - reaching, extending, and gliding out front. They look beautiful and smooth.

The athletes get excited that they reduced their number of strokes from 10 down to 8. They probably raised their hands to tell the coach the good news, and the coach probably high-fived them. But, here is the problem: the coach never told them about rate. No one timed their turnover. Now, instead of taking 1 second per stroke, the swimmers are taking 1.5 seconds per stroke, because they are gliding out front so long on every stroke.

By the end of the clinic, their equation looks like this:

$$8 \text{ strokes} \times \frac{1.5 \text{ seconds}}{\text{stroke}} = 12 \text{ seconds}$$

Yikes! They became slower. They left the clinic thinking they became faster, but they were never given the full picture.

It kills me to watch, because they were led to believe they would improve their swimming by focusing only on reducing their number of strokes.

They won't realize this for a while. In fact, for many they will never quite understand, as time goes by, what they ended up doing wrong after the clinic. I hope this book gets into the hands of everyone who has experienced that, because I want to tell them that they did nothing wrong. The problem was that they were never given the full picture. They were only given half the equation and led to believe that was all they needed to be on their way to swimming stardom.

The bottom line is that you cannot improve the NUMBER OF STROKES side of the equation by gliding out front. That is NOT what a swimmer does.

Actually, I take that statement partially back. Gliding does serve one particular group of swimmers quite well. It serves the swimmer who would like to enjoy the sport either for exercise or for the purpose of learning to swim to be able to survive through a triathlon, or as a friend of mine once said, "Swimming is good to know in case your boat sinks." Anyone who is not focused on time, and who simply wants the enjoyment of being able to swim (or is a survivalist), will benefit wonderfully from stretching out his or her stroke. It is less taxing and simple to do. It is also a healthy, low-impact exercise.

However, if you are a swimmer who wants to be competitive, then you have to hang with me for a while longer to find out how to reduce the number of strokes you take without adversely affecting your rate. That is coming up, but first I want to show you example #2.

Example 2: For this example you have to imagine a completely different scenario:

Now you are at an age-group swim meet, and the adorable 8 and Unders are on the blocks for the 25 Yard Freestyle. Their goggles are on crooked, their suits are too big for them, and they are ready to dive (or jump) in and give it their all. They have so much energy stored up that they are like a wind-up toy, and that is exactly what they look like when they race down the pool. Their arms spin at warp speed. They take about a million strokes to get to the other end. It is the cutest thing ever!

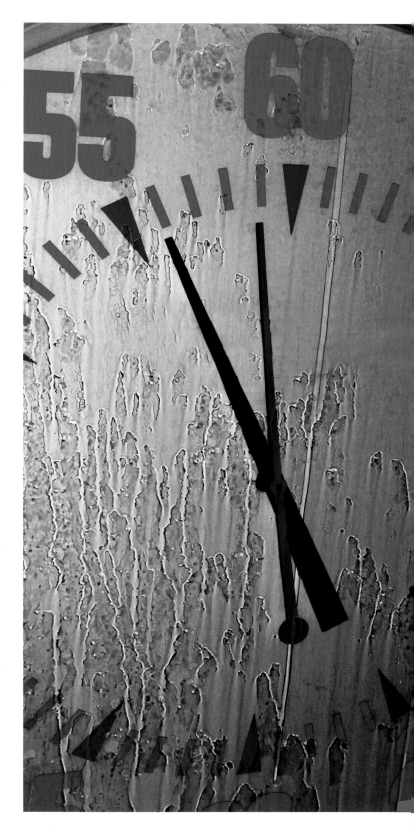

Here is what their equation looks like:

$$15 \text{ strokes} \times \frac{0.8 \text{ seconds}}{\text{stroke}} = 12 \text{ seconds}$$

The great effort that was just put forth by this little swimmer ends up not paying off. The time is slower. Even though the rate side of the equation was reduced, the number of strokes went up significantly, because the arms never "held" the water. This scenario can be likened to a car's wheels spinning on ice.

** Please Note** The numbers I am using in these examples are chosen for simplicity purposes only. In Chapter 7, the actual stroke count and rate numbers we see in the top swimmers are explained.

Most people reading this book will fall into the category of Example #1, but Example #2 is important to understand. The reason? Because learning to "hold" the water is critical. We are about to discuss what that means. If you are paying close attention to words, then "critical" is your clue that we are getting closer to discussing the 20% of things that take us 80% of the way to optimizing both factors in our equation.

Summary for Chapter 2

1. There are only two ways to get faster in swimming:
   a) take fewer strokes
   b) turnover more quickly

2. The equation to remember:
   (Number of Strokes) x (Rate) = Time

3. We must reduce one or both of the factors in order to improve our time.

4. Be careful to pay attention to both factors when making a stroke change, because they are not always independent of each other. By lowering one factor you may end up increasing the other factor to the point where the total time is adversely affected.

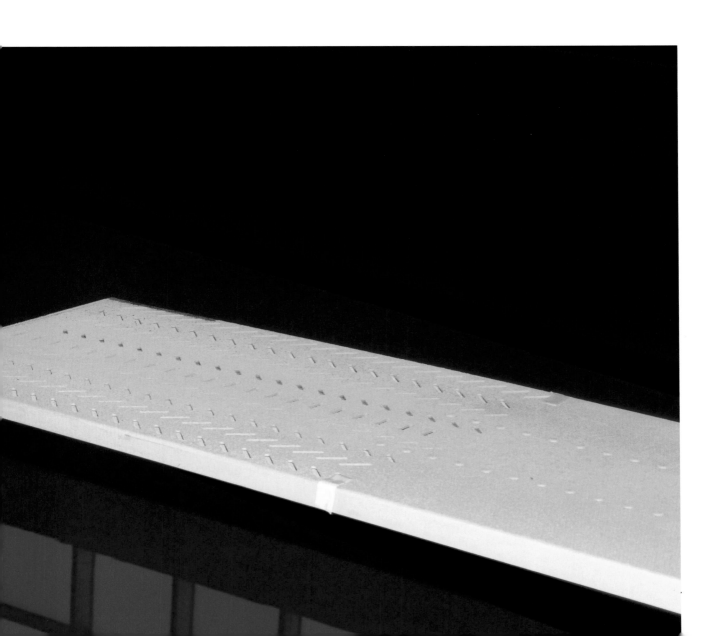

Chapter 3
The Vital Element Revealed
a case to prove it

Now that you understand the equation from Chapter 2 and the fact that both the number of strokes and the rate of turnover are important, we are going to move on to a chapter that takes so many twists and turns that it is difficult to introduce. It is an extremely important chapter, however, because not only does it reveal the most vital element in swimming, but also it presents an argument to prove the claim. To begin, let's introduce the topic of water and what swimmers are to do with it.

The topic of water

Water is interesting. It is a medium midway between air and a solid object. Picture yourself trying to grab air. You cannot hold it. You cannot pull yourself forward (remember how you tried to fly off your back porch as a kid and went nowhere?) Now, picture yourself holding onto a solid object that is anchored in the ground, like a sign post. If you hold the post with your hand, you can pull your body forward. Your hand stays locked on the post, and your body moves in the direction you pulled. Your hand stayed; your body moved.

In essence, water has more substance (viscosity/thickness) than air, but it is not nearly as solid as an object that is anchored. The interesting part about water is that, depending on what we do with our body, the water can be manipulated in different ways. We can apply pressure to it so that it feels somewhat solid, or we can slip through it like a seal.

How to work with the water

As swimmers we actually want to work with the water in both of those ways simultaneously. First, consider that swimming is a three-dimensional sport. We have a depth component in addition to the lateral and forward/backward components of surface sports. Because of this depth component, swimming is unique. There are two beautiful dynamics going on at the same time. One dynamic is taking place on the surface of the water, and the other is taking place deeper in the water, where our arm is pulling.

Let's first talk about the part that takes place deeper in the water, where our arm is pulling. Here we want to work with the water to make it as solid as possible.

(1) Making water solid

If you have ever heard the phrase, "Wow, that person has a great feel for the water," or "Look at the hold that person has on the water," then what you were hearing was that the swimmer being observed was doing a great job of making the water below as solid as possible.

From the pool deck it looks like the swimmer is moving effortlessly, but in reality there is a ton of work going on beneath the surface. The hand/arm is anchored on the water below, pulling the body over top. Ideally, a swimmer wants to move the body forward, not the hand backward.

For all of the out-of-date elements Johnny Weissmuller wrote about in *Swimming the American Crawl,* (keeping the chest and shoulders high, and not rotating the hips) he was way ahead of his time when it came to the concept of making the water beneath him solid. Below is a beautiful description. He writes:

"Water is elusive, but you can get 'hold' of it if you know how to go after it." [1]

Another phrase he used to convey the job of holding water was "purchase power." I love it! He described how his arm would "feel for the purchase" of the water. Today we use the term "catch." The catch is essentially the very first moment that we get our hold, or feel, for the water. It happens out front. When our hand enters the water, we grab it, "catch it," "purchase it," and then stay on it - hold it. This is the part of swimming that is most like artwork.

There are a number of ways to describe the concepts of "catching" and "holding" the water. A coach once told me to envision a brick wall underneath me. He said, "Grab a hold of it, LOCK ON, and pull your body over the wall." That vision worked for me. Some coaches, however, believe this is a misrepresentation of what is going on under the water. Cecil Colwin, legendary Australian swimming coach and historian who has written a number of insightful books on technique and training, stated in his book, *Breakthrough Swimming*:

"To convey the concept of a force acting on a mass of water, the act of propulsion has been variously described as feeling for undisturbed water, anchoring the hand on a fixed spot in the water and pulling the body past it....These descriptions, strictly speaking, are inappropriate because the propulsive force is not applied against a solid or rigid resistance. Coaches should use carefully chosen words when instructing a swimmer." [2]

Allison Schmitt, *2008 Olympic Medalist*

Reducing resistance at the surface while making the water solid below.

Colwin is correct; words should be chosen carefully. Water indeed is not a rigid substance. Semantics is important, but keep in mind that a particular description may register for one person while another description turns on the light for someone else. I benefited tremendously by picturing a wall beneath me. We have much more to discuss about this concept of the "feel" and "hold" of the "elusive water," Colwin's ideas included, but for now the main take-away is to understand that there is an application of force we must place against the water with our pulling arm.

(2) Reducing resistance

While the "hold" is taking place below us, on the surface our relationship with the water is completely different. The head, torso, hips and legs should slip through the water. We do not want to feel like the water in front of us is solid. We have to move through it.

This is the part of swimming where we have been taught to think about body position, hip roll, head position, and any other technique that reduces resistance. These are definitely important aspects of swimming; however, they are purposefully neglected in this book. The reason? They are already being thoroughly discussed, and with too much emphasis. They are such hot topics that they are smothering any discussion of what really makes a competitive swimmer - the hold and pull underneath us.

A three-dimensional sport...with surface components and depth components.

The Vital Element Revealed

There! The cat's out of the bag - competitive swimming is far more about the hold and pull than it is about body position. Take a sip of that Italian roast coffee I hope you're drinking and offer a toast to Pareto, because we have just revealed 80% of swimming!

If you don't believe me, then go to a beach and watch the sunbathers wade into the water and proceed to float on their backs, soaking in the warm sun. They have a wonderful body position on top of the water - as good as I did when I swam at the Olympics. The kicker is that they are not getting anywhere. Remember, swimmers need to move forward.

Now, don't misunderstand. Body position is definitely something that the top swimmers understand and try to perfect. Scientists, coaches, and swim suit manufacturers all study the flow of water over and around the body, so I am not saying that it is not an important factor in swimming. What I am saying is that they have developed something that is far more vital - the pull. The only reason their work on body position considerations means anything is because they are tearing up the pool already with an incredible pull.

Doubters

Oh dear, I can sense the doubt from a few of you. You are just like a good friend of mine who is one of the top triathletes in his age group. He has been a student of the "glide like a fish theory" for a number of years and is very protective of it. He and I had a conversation during which he described a swim clinic he attended over a decade ago. By the end of the two-day clinic he was so convinced that swimming started and ended with body position considerations only, that he actually believed the pull under the water was a fixed force. In other words, he believed that no matter what position he held his arm he was applying the same force, so to him the pull was a moot point. At the clinic, there was no discussion about the underwater pull. My friend believed his only potential for improvement was, as he put it, "to get his entire body to go through as narrow a tube as possible," to reduce resistance.

He said he had been working on this for more than a decade. When I asked him if he has become faster, he said, "Well, no." I gave him the look that said, "You are one of the most intelligent guys I know. How in the world did you not realize something was wrong?" The very fact that he continued to work on the same thing for more than a decade that resulted in no time reduction tells me that there is a need to help triathletes (and many masters swimmers and age-groupers) to see the real picture.

Books on the market today include every detail of the swim stroke you would want to know. They are full of great information, but none of them organize the information to reveal the VITAL FEW. People who read those books are naturally going to gravitate to the aspects of technique that are most simple to apply. Those aspects will not be beneficial if you lack the foundation of a solid pull.

I am on a mission to show you the real picture of what the top swimmers do and how it relates to the equation from Chapter 2 (Number of Strokes x Rate = Time). I realize that I have to back up this claim, so let's get to that now. The following pages explain why the pull is the vital factor and why body position is not.

Reasons why the pull
is the vital factor

Reason #1: Throughout the decades the pull has been the same

When I studied underwater video and photos of the greatest swimmers throughout the last 5 decades, I noticed the critical position of the arm under the water was virtually the same. The world record holders of the '60s, '70s, and '80s did the same crucial elements of the pull as the fastest swimmers today. This, in and of itself, does not prove a thing. However, when this is contrasted with the fact that every triathlete and swimmer I know who struggles to go fast in the water employs fantastic body position technique yet none of the critical elements of the underwater hold, some conclusions can be made.

Why is not every serious swimmer and triathlete churning out a 57.4 in the 100 Meter Free like Johnny Weissmuller did? It is because Weissmuller knew how to "purchase" the water, as he said, and many athletes today have never given that a thought. Everyone is so busy trying to get through that narrow tube my friend described. It is time to take a lesson from Weissmuller and figure out how to get a hold of the "elusive" and move forward.

If Weissmuller's times are not fast enough for you, then I'll step it up a notch. Let's look at Mark Spitz. He swam a 1:52 in the 200 Meter Freestyle (Long Course) at the Munich Games, and he was lugging around a big, hairy mustache when he did that....

...And he was swimming in a nylon suit that is nothing like the space suits worn today,

...And the pike dive, which essentially stops a swimmer dead in the water, was the rage,

...And there was no talk about "pressing the T" and "swimming downhill,"

I could go on about pool technology, and that goggles were not allowed in 1972, and a number of other things, but hopefully the point has been made: you can try to get streamlined and reduce resistance all you want, but if you don't know how to hold the water beneath you, then Spitz is going to crush you with his big, hairy mustache in tow, and Weissmuller is going to embarrass you even more as he sings his Tarzan song and strokes to victory with the exact technique that would mortify students and coaches of the "body position and glide" school.

Johnny Weissmuller (a.k.a., Tarzan), *swimming with the exact stroke that earned him five Olympic gold medals and 67 world records.*

Johnny's 100 Meter Freestyle (long course meters) world record: 57.4.

Photo courtesy of The International Swimming Hall of Fame.

Reason #2: The Law Of Diminishing Returns

This is one of the most famous laws in all of Economics (sorry Pareto). It states that:

> "We will get less and less extra output, when we add additional doses of an input, while holding other inputs fixed."
> *(Credit: Wikipedia)*

This law relates to our swimming situation in that once a swimmer is **already horizontal** in the water, then:

> We will get less and less extra output
> *output here being "swimming faster"*
>
> when we add additional doses of an input
> *additional doses of an input being, "trying to get more horizontal in the water"*
>
> while holding other inputs fixed
> *other inputs held fixed being "keeping the crummy pull fixed."*

This is exactly what is happening in the triathlon world and much of the swimming world. Ninety-five percent of the swimmers and triathletes I know (professionals included) are showing up to practice and working on diminishing returns.

How can this be? Why do so many people continue to work on elements of stroke technique that do not give them significant returns while completely ignoring the vital aspects? I am not 100% certain, but I have a good guess as to how the story panned out. It goes something like this:

Top swimmers and coaches have always searched for ways to get faster. Races are won and lost in increments of hundredths of seconds, so part of the study of swimming throughout the years has been to identify areas in which every gain, no matter how big or small, can be made. In the 1990s body position became the new rage. I remember it clearly. I was swimming in Michigan with the Clarenceville Swim Club, and rumor made its way across the country that a man named Bill Boomer was working with the Stanford swimmers on how to use the body core to improve swimming power, efficiency, and speed. It was mysterious to me; phrases such as "pressing the T" were being thrown around, and I had no idea what it meant. I just knew it was big stuff if Stanford was buying into it.

Luckily I was busy working on other glaring weaknesses, like not wimping out when my coach told me to swim 6 x 100 on 8:00 ALL OUT.

Anyway, what happened was, while body core concepts were being touted in the swimming world, simultaneously there was a growing need, thus a new market opportunity, for swim instruction within the triathlon and masters swimming world. Swim clinics began to sprout-up around the country, and the focus was this new and exciting revelation about the body core and the applications of it that would improve speed and power. Masters swimmers and triathletes signed up in droves, believing they were finally handed the ticket to swimming prowess. The problem was that every other element of swim technique was virtually ignored, particularly the most vital one.

It is natural that this happened. New information breeds a flurry of enthusiasm. At some point though, a leader must emerge to tame the excitement. A level-headed analysis requires that we **understand how new information fits within the overall scope of our mission**. Businesses and other types of organizations create mission statements and vision statements exactly for this reason – to guide decision making and to be constantly reminded of the core of their existence. Otherwise it is very easy to go astray, chasing rabbits. We have a limited amount of time, energy, and resources, so the majority of our working efforts had better be spent on activities that impact the bottom line.

This point was driven home in 2001 while I was touring a Mrs. T's Pierogie's manufacturing plant in Pennsylvania. As I stood in awe, witnessing thousands of pierogies streaming down the conveyer belt, I shouted over the noise of the machines to ask the president of the company who was standing nearby, "This is a lot of pierogies! Do you make anything other than pierogies?"

His response, shouting back, was, "Well, one time we tried to make ravioli...but then we realized after a little while that we are just really good at making pierogies."

Mrs. T's knew the key to their success - pierogies. They tried something new - ravioli, but they saw that the ravioli business was diverting too much energy and resources away from what really made them successful.

With regards to your swimming, I assume that your vision/mission is to move forward, and at a pretty good clip at that. The core of your existence, if you are to be competitive in the sport, is TIME (remember # strokes x rate from Chapter 2). Be careful not to chase rabbits (such as pursuing a reduction in stroke count without checking how it affects your TIME). Every choice you make needs to effectively support your vision.

The question then becomes, "How do we know when new information supports our mission or diverts resources away from it?" The answer: We will not know, or at minimum we will be taking a wild guess...UN-

LESS we delve deeper into understanding all that is involved in the making of something. In other words, for you to take charge of your swimming goals and ensure that your efforts in the pool provide a certain level of return (rather than diminishing returns), you must understand what goes into the making of an authentic competitive swimmer. You must become what one of my new favorite authors, Matthew B. Crawford, in his book, *Shop Class as Soulcraft*, calls a "craftsperson." Crawford, a motorcycle mechanic with a PhD in Political Philosophy, sways the reader to value the skills of the manual trades worker (i.e., plumbers, electricians, mechanics) as much as the "soft knowledge" skills of business executives.

Among his many arguments, not the least of which is the skills of the manual trades will never become obsolete, is that a craftsperson, because of his/her understanding of the production narrative, does not discard things that are perfectly serviceable in a relentless pursuit of the new.

In swimming, what if we all became craftsmen and craftswomen? If we really knew what went into the making of a fast swimmer, then our laps up and down the pool could be designed to effectively support any goal. We would know which elements of stroke technique impact the bottom line and which ones do not.

As mentioned in the Introduction, I want to show you the real picture of what "swimmers" do. I want to show you the production narrative so that your efforts in the pool provide you with a significant return rather than a diminishing return. That is coming up in the following chapters but first let's move on the third point about why the pull is the most vital aspect of swimming...

Reason #3: The Theoretical Square Law

The implications of this law are found in many textbooks written on swimming. The most practical explanation is found in, *The Science of Swimming*, by James Counsilman:

"The Theoretical Square Law: The resistance a body creates in water (or any fluid or gas) varies approximately with the square of its velocity. To illustrate this fact, let us use an airplane going 100 mph and say that it creates 1000 pounds of resistance. When the airplane doubles its speed to 200 mph, it does not simply double its resistance; rather, the resistance increases by four times, or to 4000 pounds. If the plane increases its speed to 300 mph, it now increases its resistance by nine times. This law also applies to the swimmer's speed and resistance in the water." [3]

The important word here is "square." Remember from math class that "squared" means "to the second power." This is not the same as doubling. The Theoretical Square Law is important to understand with regards to swimming, because as we increase our speed, the resistance grows at an exponential rate, not at a rate proportional to the output of power.

This means that when a swimmer is traveling at faster speeds, then resistance becomes more of an issue. We have the quintessential question here: Which came first...the chicken or the egg? If, in the case of swimming, we want to know which comes first - forward propulsion or reducing resistance - the answer is provided by The Theoretical Square Law: Moving forward comes FIRST. Only when we are traveling at greater speeds does resistance become an exponentially concerning factor.

Think about The Tour De France. When does the peloton break up and stay broken up? Not on the flat sections where the speed is fast, but rather in the mountains where the speed is slower. If we think about the Theoretical Square Law in this situation, then it makes perfect sense. The cyclists leading the pack on the flat sections are traveling upward of 30 mph in many places - the resistance for

Cycling peloton   Source: Wikimedia Commons

them is massive. Every other cyclist can tuck behind the leaders and dodge the resistance. Once the mountains appear, however, and the speeds slow down, the resistance for the leaders is much less. This is when strength becomes important, and when we see the best cyclists shine. No longer is the advantage so great by drafting, because the steeper the incline, the slower the speed - and the slower the speed, the less resistance the lead cyclists are facing (exponentially!). In the mountains, every cyclist is riding on a more level playing field, so to speak.

Going back to the Theoretical Square Law as it applies to swimming - reducing resistance becomes a relevant concern only if we are moving forward. Swimmers should invest their energy, focus, and time on developing elements of the stroke that first and foremost provide the propulsive forces. You should spend 80% of your time working on these propulsive forces. The top swimmers are doing this.

Still some skeptics

No way! Some of you are still skeptical?! Seriously? Even though we just finished talking about the Theoretical Square Law and the Law of Diminishing Returns, pierogies, and everything else? Fine then, I am totally game for this drag 'em down, knock 'em out boxing match. Here are a few more arguments to back up my claim that the PULL is the most vital part of swimming:

First, Most Importantly, Numero Uno:
OUR PULL dictates both the NUMBER OF STROKES we take and the RATE at which we take those strokes. No other part of swimming has a greater impact on those two factors.

Next, a Crazy but Valid Point:
Think about the physical attributes of great swimmers. What is the most distinctive look of their bodies? It is the shoulders and the lat muscles; they have broad shoulders and distinctive V-shaped bodies, right? Well, common sense would tell me that if swimmers are supposedly most concerned with reducing resistance, then someone should tell them to taper down those shoulders and lats a bit. Oh, and I also would like to know how they got that look in the first place. Something tells me they did not get it from doing 6-count extension and hip rotation drills all day long.

Third, going back to the visual of the beach-goers floating on the water:
I want to point out that you can get a great body position very quickly and with next to no physical effort. Those vacationers, believe me, are not stressing themselves out while they lay there on the water. In fact, most swimmers I have seen, whether age-groupers, masters swimmers, or triathletes, have body positions as good as I had. If the critical aspect of swimming fast pertained to body position primarily, then the whole world would be streaming through the water at great speeds, because everyone could develop it quickly and with little effort.

Lastly, Watch Out...Here Comes the Left Hook:
If you are a triathlete, masters swimmer, or age-grouper who has worked excessively on body position, and not on the pull, then I am willing to guess that your warm-up speed in practice is not much different from your main set speed. I see it all the time, especially in adults. They dive in for warm-up and go a 1:27 on their first 100 yards. Then when the main set comes along, and they are supposed to be working hard at their repeat 100s, they crank out 1:30s. Ouch. That is not how it is supposed to work.

Great swimmers have a variety of speeds, including warm-up speeds, aerobic training speeds, threshold speeds, lactate speeds, and pure sprint speeds. They are able to vary their speed based on how much force they choose to put into their propulsion; it is not based on whether or not they choose to improve their body position on the threshold set more than on the warm-up.

My opponent, although dazed and confused, fires back

This argument is winding down, but I still see there is one last bit of fight left in my opponent.

He/she rebuts my points with, "Come on! We cannot expect someone to swim with their feet dragging on the bottom of the pool." I say, "Fair enough. Allow those people the opportunity to address body position first." I'll concede that no one should have to struggle through the water vertically, nor should any observer have to suffer through watching that, but I give them one swim session to get it done. If it takes longer than that, then something is wrong. (Very new beginners see "Side Note" below).

The last point my opponent brings up is that the pull is too advanced to explain to new swimmers. I would say, "Oh, this is going to be fun...please let me stand in the room when you tell them that."

TKO

Ok, I hope you are getting my sense of humor, and I also thank you for your patience while I debated my imaginary opponent. I am going to end this section of the book by saying that was a "TKO" and raising my own arm in the air. And I don't even like boxing. (P.S. For those of you who don't know what a TKO is, it is Technical Knockout, and my opponent wants out of this bloody match.)

The good news and the bad news

I only have a little bit of bad news: the pull definitely takes more effort, more time, and is more difficult to learn than every other aspect of swimming (this is partly why it is neglected at clinics). The position we must hold under the water does not simulate anything we do in life, so we are teaching a muscle memory that is completely foreign.

The good news is that it is not rocket science. It is 100% do-able! Any swimmer who chooses to put forth effort on the pull will not only see improvement in his/her swimming times, but will also get toned, strong swimmer arms. If that effort is concentrated and non-wavering (in other words, if you keep it slow and easy for the first few weeks and do not bail out on stroke technique in order to keep up with your buddies in the lane) then you are going to see the first signs of improvement within three to six weeks. This is assuming

you get to the pool at least three days a week (amount of yardage is not so important as long as every stroke is focused) and do the tubing exercises at least three days a week (these exercises are explained in Chapter 6).

Wipe your brow

Ok, phew. That is over. I hope you're learning something about swimming, but if not, then you must at least be learning about economics and laws of resistance. Nothing wrong with that.

Side note to new swimmers: For those of you who are new to swimming, or who have a natural aversion to the water, you will need to spend some time simply getting to know the water. Establishing the correct body position is easy, but learning to relax is sometimes not. Body position is important for you during this time, as is learning how to breathe. Work on keeping your head neutral in the water rather than lifting it (which many new swimmers do because of panicking).

Here is the great news: while you are getting comfortable in the water for a few weeks, you can train out of the water developing your pull. This is explained in Chapter 6. The same chapter also explains one in-water exercise that will be very manageable for you. Then, once you feel comfortable in the water and are able to concentrate on technique, you will be ahead of the game in terms of strength, flexibility, and muscle memory.

Summary for Chapter 3

1. Swimming is a three-dimensional sport. We have a job to do at the surface of the water, and we have a different job to do beneath us.

2. Beneath us the water must feel solid. We lock on to the water with our hand and pull our body forward.

3. At the surface, we must slip through the water. We find ways to position our body to reduce resistance.

4. Body position is important, but it is not the separating factor between the best swimmers and those who struggle to go fast.

5. The key to swimming fast, above all else, is developing a great pull.

You may have noticed that the 80/20 Rule, The Law Of Diminishing Returns, and the principles behind mission/vision statements all relate to understanding massive amounts of information, organizing it, and staying focused on the pieces that have the biggest impact. This is the crux of the book - to point out how these thought processes can be a launching pad for your success in swimming as well as other areas of your life.

Chapter 4

Fluid Dynamics and Theories of Propulsion
the challenges and the beauty

Hopefully now you are convinced the underwater pull should take its place as King of the Hill in swimming. I know that once I started laying my bets on it, I made four Olympic teams. There is so much depth and potential in all that is below us when we swim, and I am excited that we are now nearing the part of the book that dives into this *third dimension.*

Before we get to the details that describe the pull and how to develop it, we have just a little more work to do on understanding the big picture of swimming; we will draw from it to make all the puzzle pieces fit. This final part of the big picture requires that we revisit the topic of water, but this time from a scientific angle - particularly with regards to the study of fluid dynamics. Every textbook on swimming technique includes a significant piece on fluid dynamics as it relates to propulsion, and it is, without fail, the distinguishing topic that gives the book its reputation. Unfortunately, it is also the most laborious, scientific section of the book, and for this reason it holds the attention of very few readers.

For a coach or athlete to grasp the concepts of "flow analysis," "vortex patterns," and "drag/lift forces" is no small task, so, as was alluded to already in this book, there is a tendency for readers to gravitate to sections of the book that are manageable (ie: body position, hip rotation, head position). Since I have opened a can of worms by convincing you that the underwater pull is the most vital aspect of the stroke, I feel obliged to present the theories on swimming propulsion in terms that are not only understandable, but also that frame the sport on an entirely new level for you.

You are finally going to understand the origins of so much of what you have heard from fellow athletes, coaches, and even the guy in the lane next to you at the health club who offers his two cents on how you should pull. If you have heard contradicting information, there is good reason; it is because the paradigms on swimming propulsion theory have shifted throughout the years, almost at the moment the swimming world was finally getting comfortable with the previous one. This is due to the nature of the medium in which our sport is contested - water. Water complicates things. Cecil Colwin explains it in *Swimming Dynamics*:

"What happens to the water when we swim? The answer is we don't exactly know.... Biomechanists claim to be able to calculate the forces that swimmers develop in the water, but the trouble with these studies is that they depend on the premise of "essentially still water." Water doesn't obediently stand still while forces act upon it. Consequently, some studies may well be flawed because they are based on the mechanic of solids rather than those of fluid behavior." [1]

Colwin continues…

….Moreover, prominent fluid dynamicists, when asked whether the flow reactions to human swimming propulsion could be analyzed by computer simulation, expressed the opinion that the rapidly changing body configurations of human swimmers almost defy complete analysis." [2]

What does this mean for us? It means that we take this big picture understanding that a human being moving through water is a bugger to analyze, and put that understanding in our back pocket as we read about the four main theories of propulsion that have prevailed, at one time or another, during the past 50+ years. Below is a short synopsis of each:

1. The first and most logical explanation of what was taking place under the water centered around Newton's Third Law - for every action there is an equal and opposite reaction. Swimming theorists believed that the arm and hand acted as a "paddle" that pulled straight back, thus the equal and opposite reaction being that the swimmer moved forward. Simple enough. It makes perfect sense. Or does it?

2. In the 1960s, the man credited with being perhaps the most pioneering mind in swimming history, Doc Counsilman (coach of Mark Spitz at Indiana University), noted that the hand does not take a path straight back; rather, he showed that the great swimming champions employed a pattern that looked like an inverted question mark. Many of us know it as the "S" pull.

Newton's Third Law for swimming propulsion theory was subsequently scrapped, and the argument was made that the inverted question mark pull was a more logical explanation due to the nature of fluid dynamics. Essentially, the theorists claimed that the arm could not simply pull/push straight back, because once the swimmer's hand/arm (the "paddle") began to apply force, the water moved. Once the water moved (as the paddle progressed through the length of the stroke), then less and less force could be applied upon that already moving water. In essence, Newton's Third Law stood true when considering forces applied to a solid, but not so much when applied to a fluid.

Doc explained that the swimmer must constantly search for new, "still" water in order to effectively apply force, thus the sculling movements of the "S" pull became the focus of research. Both Doc and a gentleman named Ernie Maglischo literally "wrote the books" on this new discovery, likening the effect of the sculling motion to an airplane propeller and wing. In Ernie's book, *Swimming Faster*, published in 1982, and in Doc's book, *The New Science of Swimming*, published in 1994, there are detailed explanations of lift forces, drag forces, and the Bernoulli Principle of fluid dynamics.

Cecil Colwin, in *Swimming Into the 21st Century*, also acknowledged the discovery:

"Counsilman's study showed that, in all the swimming strokes, the pull does not follow a straight line but is composed of short sculling motions, or impulses, that change direction as the hand moves in a curved path across the line of a swimmer's forward movement." [3]

However, while Colwin agreed that the hand does indeed take a curvilinear path, and not a straight line, he published his own theory for why this sculling motion provides forward movement and how the swimmer is to manage it.

3. Colwin introduced to the swimming world the concept of the vortex. What is a vortex? I asked the same question. Luckily for us, Colwin describes it quite well in his book, *Swimming Dynamics.*

"A vortex is a mass of fluid that rotates about an axis....A vortex is a form of kinetic energy, the energy of motion. A shed vortex represents the energy produced by a swimmer and "given" to the water. In fact, when you see vortices produced by the swimmer in the water, you are actually looking at the swimmer's propulsion....Vortices often become visible to the underwater viewer when a swimmer is moving at top speed and accidentally entraps air into the stroke.

....In 1984, I presented a study on the significance of vortex flow reactions in the swimming stroke. Later I was surprised to hear my report referred to by biomechanists as the 'vortex theory of propulsion.' This is not a theory but a physical fact - there exists no other way of producing propulsion in a fluid.

....Without the resistive friction provided by vortex turbulence within a fluid, no tractive force would be provided. This is as true for swimmers as it is for ocean liners. In fact, all forms of propulsion through a fluid, whether by airplanes, fish, birds, flying insects, and so on, depend on resistive forces provided by vortices." [4]

Colwin ultimately pioneers a worthy explanation of swimming propulsion by connecting vortex science with his observations from the pool deck. His work yields an interesting description of how a swimmer should feel for the flow of water at various phases of the stroke, and he explains how the swimmer becomes a skilled "shaper of the flow."

4. Finally, the most recent text comes from Ernie Maglischo, and in it he back-paddles to the 1960s. In *Swimming Fastest* (2003) he **retracts** his own theory (the airplane propeller/wing, lift, drag, and Bernoulli Principle explanations written about in #2 previously) that was published in *Swimming Faster*. The reason for the retraction? The point was made that a boundary layer is present on airplane wings that is not present on the human hand and arm, and this boundary layer is critical for Bernoulli's principle to apply. Therefore, the explanation that the human hand/arm acts in the same way as an airplane propeller or wing could not hold up.

Below is Ernie's retraction, found in *Swimming Fastest*. He also comments on Colwin's vortex theory of propulsion:

"I now believe that some of the information I presented on stroke mechanics in previous editions was incorrect. My primary purpose with this edition is to correct that information.

....I consider the evidence that Bernoulli's Principle is not involved in swimming propulsion quite compelling. I also believe that the evidence currently available does not support the notion that propulsion is the result of

forming and shedding vortices. In my opinion, Newton's Third Law of motion, the law of action-reaction, offers the most likely explanation for human swimming propulsion....I believe that the act of pushing water in a **predominantly** backward direction creates the propulsive force that accelerates a swimmer's body forward." [5]

The key word in the sentence above is "predominantly." Maglischo does not boomerang all the way back to the pre-1960s theory that subscribed to Newton's Third Law. He believes there is a presence of lift and drag forces still in play and that the backward push has a **diagonal** component to it.

Stay tuned for the latest though. Ernie learned from his past mistake, and this, combined with the fact that we do not know exactly how water reacts when we pull, led him to make a disclaimer in *Swimming Fastest*:

"While this is the theory of propulsion that I have come to accept after several years of study, I cannot guarantee that it is, in all respects, an accurate explanation of human propulsive mechanisms. At the present time, however, it seems to be the most logical explanation based on the available evidence." [6]

What should we do with this information?

Even in consideration of Ernie's disclaimer and the recognized limits of scientific analysis in general, there are numerous insights contained in each theory described above. So, let's take all of the great work that Maglischo, Counsilman, and Colwin have done and grab bits and pieces from it to craft a beautiful, powerful swim stroke. We will do this in the next chapter.

Summary for Chapter 4

1. Scientists are not yet able to fully analyze the propulsive forces of a swimmer.

2. The four main theories on swimming propulsion include principles centered around:

a. **Newton's Third Law** - push straight back to move straight forward.

b. **Lift/drag, Bernoulli's Principle** - employ an "S" pattern to find still water.

c. **Vortex Theory of Propulsion** - resistive friction provided by vortex turbulence within a fluid. Shape the flow of water.

d. **Newton's Third Law with a diagonal component**- push back with a diagonal component.

3. Each theory provides clues as to how to work with the water to gain propulsive power.

Above: a series of vortices produced by a swimmer's kick

Chapter 5
The Underwater Pull
vital elements of the vital element

We are building something here, and the foundation has just been laid. Each one of us, no matter what our goals in swimming, should have a firm grasp of the big picture and the choices that can be made. Understanding fluid dynamics, theories on propulsion, and the equation from Chapter 2 provides a solid footing from which you may build your swim stroke.

With the big picture understanding now in hand, you are ready to look closely at the underwater pull, and learn the vital elements of this Vital Element. Yes, you read that correctly - there are vital elements to the Vital Element. One truth here is that technique cannot be boxed. Individuals have unique levels of strength, flexibility, and other attributes - even including a natural rhythm.

If you look at 10 different swimming champions you will see variances in the stroke mechanics in each one of them; however, without fail, they all eventually make their way to the critical elements. For instance, Ian Thorpe of Australia - Olympic champion in the 400 Freestyle in 2000 - was so strong in his upper body that he could begin the critical elements of the underwater pull with his arm fully extended, but Brooke Bennett, the women's gold medalist in the 400 Freestyle at those same Olympics, swam completely differently - her stroke was short and "choppy," and her arm never came close to extending before she got a hold of the water below.

My goal has been, and continues to be in this chapter, to give you an understanding of the things you cannot do without. Once you know those few things, then be brave - believe in your own style. Never sacrifice, however, the vital few. Every decision you make with regards to technique needs to support those critical elements.

This chapter is filled with pages of photographs to visually present the key aspects of the pull. The underwater pictures are actually the inspiration for this book. I hope you enjoy.

The first Vital Element of the pull revealed:

Some of the fastest swimmers in the world have awkward looking recoveries, kicks, breathing patterns, and other quirks. They are however, doing two things amazingly well. The first of these is shown to the right.

Are you doing this? If not, then the rest of your pull is rendered virtually ineffective.

One of the two Vital Elements of the pull is the **HIGH-ELBOW POSITION during the early phase of the stroke.** The high-elbow position you see to the right has ALWAYS been one of the separating factors between swimming champions and those who are stumped as to why their times are not improving.

Allison Schmitt, NCAA Champion and 2008 Olympic Medalist

Right now is a perfect time to look at the underwater photos that span the decades so that you can see how this critical element has never been missing in the strokes of the top swimmers:

Mike Troy, *1960 Olympic Gold Medalist*
Above photos courtesy: Indiana University, Counsilman Center for the Science of Swimming

Mark Spitz, *1972 Olympic Gold Medalist*

Sheila Taormina, *1996 Olympic Gold Medalist,*
Smallest swimmer to win Olympic Gold since 1920

Allison Schmitt, *2008 Olympic Bronze Medalist,*
NCAA Champion

The high-elbow position was even present in Johnny Weissmuller's stroke. Although there are no underwater photos to prove it, Weissmuller writes a clear description of it in his book, *Swimming the American Crawl*:

"The upper arm should be raised, the elbow pointing upward to permit the forearm to hang down almost perpendicularly, and then go forward on a sort of pendulum swing."[1]

Are you starting to see why he could post a 57.4 in the 1920s, with a body position far less streamlined than any swimmer or triathlete today? He understood the high-elbow.

What is required to develop the high-elbow?

There are two physical components required for the high-elbow position: **Strength and Flexibility.**

1. Strength: as was mentioned in Chapter 3, swimmers have distinctive "V" shaped bodies and broad shoulders. Let's look at the broad shoulders first.

The reason why a swimmer appears to have broad shoulders is due to a very well developed deltoid muscle. The deltoid sits on the lateral side of the shoulder. It is the muscle that holds the upper arm high in the water, with the elbow pointing upward as Weissmuller explains.

If you stand on dry land and hold the high-elbow position, the deltoid will start to feel a burn quickly. It is an extremely awkward position, unlike anything we normally do during our day; therefore, this strength is only developed with specific focus.

Deltoid

Peter Vanderkaay, *2008 Olympic Gold Medalist*

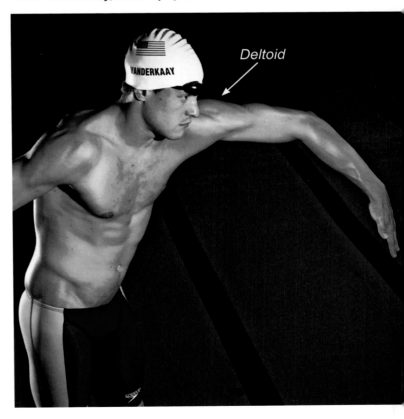

Deltoid

Peter Vanderkaay, 2008 Olympic Gold Medalist

To explain it a bit further, think of the arm as two levers. The first lever is the upper arm, from the shoulder to the elbow, and as you know now, it is critical for the high-elbow position under the water. The tendency is to drop the entire lever when fatigue sets in. Huge mistake! This is why we must stay focused and slow things down while we build this strength.

The second lever is the forearm that Weissmuller explained should "hang down perpendicularly." The hand is also an important part of it. This lever (forearm and hand), is what "holds" the water. Each of the four theories on propulsion acknowledges that the forearm and hand are responsible for the application of force that must be placed against the water. The theories diverge on the finer points of how to continually work with the water to maintain the resistive force, but they all promote a downward facing forearm during the early phase of the stroke.

We are going to come back to lever 2 again soon, because it is the key to the second Vital Element of the pull. However, I want to finish explaining the other physical component that is required for developing the high-elbow:

2. Flexibility: the high-elbow position during the early phase of the stroke requires that a swimmer not only be uniquely strong in his or her shoulders, but also uniquely flexible.

A responsive, strong muscle is not one that is tight and bound. If you look closely at the photos in this chapter, you will see a medial rotation of the shoulder against the chin/cheek area. For years I took this medial rotation for granted, believing it was simple to do. When I started coaching swim clinics, I was shocked to find the majority of people at the clinics could not rotate their shoulders toward their chin. It was then that I realized this movement had to be trained.

For this shoulder rotation to take place, the muscles surrounding the scapula (wing bone) must release to allow the upper arm (our first lever) to jut forward toward the chin.

Look at the sequence of photos on this page. They depict 1960 Olympic Gold Medalist, Mike Troy, in the front phase of the swim stroke. Take note of how the shoulder is rotated next to the chin/cheek area (medial shoulder rotation). Also note the forward extension of the scapula (wing bone).

There are many things we can do to develop the strength and flexibility required for a high elbow. They are difficult at first, but always remember that tissue does respond. If you keep working at it, you will see the gains. The next chapter includes exercises on how to develop this.

Let's go back to the second lever now - the forearm that hangs down perpendicularly from the high-elbow during the early phase of the swim stroke. As was mentioned, the function of this lever is to "hold" the water.

If a swimmer is doing a good job of holding the water, then the lat muscles in our back come into play. The lats are actually the muscles that work with the body core to pull the swimmer forward. Lat muscles, however, only play part of the role with regards to the second lever...

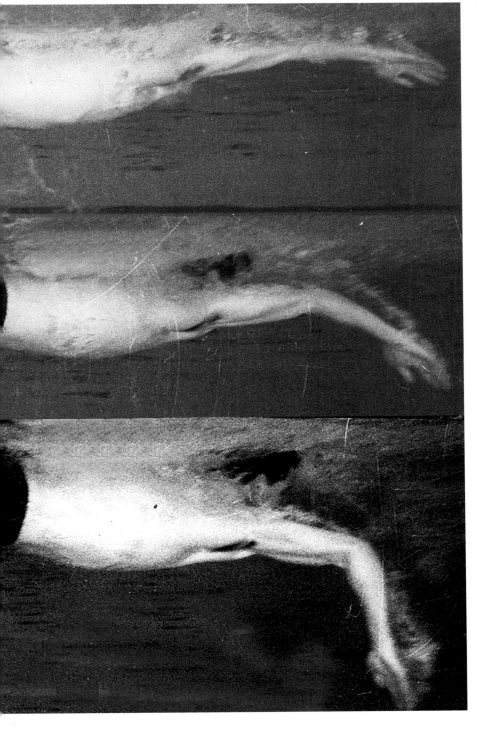

Mike Troy, 1960 Olympic Gold Medalist. Photo courtesy: Indiana University, Counsilman Center for the Science of Swimming

Ask any female swimmer if she enjoys shopping for a Homecoming or Prom dress, and she will tell you that it is nearly impossible to find one that zips up her back because of her lats.

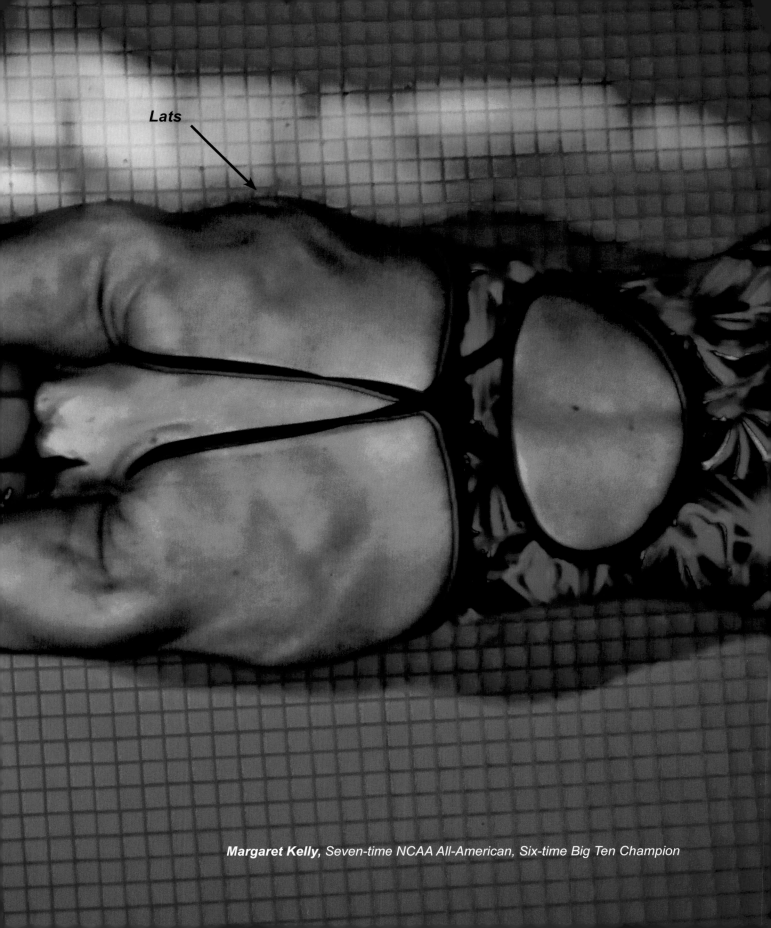

Lats

Margaret Kelly, *Seven-time NCAA All-American, Six-time Big Ten Champion*

The second Vital Element of the pull revealed

Far more rewarding than anything else you will gain from swimming is developing a FEEL for the water. This is the second and final Vital Element of the pull revealed. It has everything to do with the forearm and hand, fluid dynamics, propulsion, and the application of force against the "elusive." It is the most beautiful part about swimming.

It is said to be the gift of only the talented. Not so. Rather it belongs to any person who is thoughtful and patient, like a craftsperson or an artist - someone who is willing to put aside the sales pitches in order to study and understand what real swimmers have mastered.

This is our tao, our method, our way. Scientists have sent rockets to the moon, but they are at a loss to definitively say how our bodies are sent to the other side of the pool. How could we, therefore, come to any conclusion other than this aspect of propulsion is the critical, separating factor in our amazing sport?

TAO
the way, a method, a technique

How to describe it

While we may approach the high-elbow position in a mechanical way (it is a function of strength and flexibility), this element of FEEL has no tolerance for science, mechanics, or reasoning. It is a swimmer's sixth sense, or at minimum it is a strange cousin to the normal sense of "feel" with which we are all familiar.

To begin understanding it, the theories on propulsion we have reviewed provide wonderful clues as to what this sense of feel entails. Which strikes a chord with you? I give a nod to them all:

Cecil Colwin, in his vortex theory of propulsion, thoughtfully describes how the energy produced by a swimmer is "given" to the water. He makes us want to look for our own vortices - the columns of kinetic energy we produce which are visible if air is entrapped by the propulsive limb. I tried to see the vortices from my kick once and almost threw my neck out as I swirled around to look back. Not recommended.

However, what about wrapping our minds around feeling the "resistive friction" and "tractive forces" that Colwin shares with us? It would be a massive mental shift perhaps, but **what if you stopped thinking about reducing resistance for a while and started thinking instead about increasing resistance for the sake of traction?** The top swimmers are doing this.

Give it some consideration. Your greatest breakthroughs will come when you are most brave and step away from your comfort zone and old habits.

Doc Counsilman taught us to steer away from the moving water that is continuously

... what if you stopped think-ing about reducing resistance for a while and started thinking instead about increasing resistance for the sake of traction?

Allison Schmitt, *NCAA Champion and Olympic Medalist, gaining traction on the water.*

created throughout the pull. He said that a swimmer must search for "still" water. Where is that still water, you may ask? Well, it is not too far away; you need not do a far-sweeping "S" pull pattern searching for something that is right in front of you. Short sculling motions or "impulses" are all that is necessary. These are small pitch and angle changes of your hand and forearm that no coach can describe. Your patience and craftsmanship is the only way to master the impulses.

These are most important during the front half of your pull. The feel of "traction" must begin with the catch. Be cognizant - from the catch to the finish of the stroke the number of impulses/sculls (directional changes of the hand) should not exceed three.

Also, please note that the impulses must take you in a FORWARD direction. Be conscious of this. You may be in the water feeling the resistive forces like a champ, but if they are not applied in such a way as to move you FORWARD then you are no better off than before you started reading this book.

Ernie Maglischo must have realized that people were taking the "S-pull" a bit too literally, sweeping laterally with such great effort that the they threw common sense (the need to move forward) right out the window. Now he chooses his words more carefully. He simplifies everything again. Does his description below connect most with you because of the simplicity?

"I believe that the act of pushing water in a predominantly backward direction creates the propulsive force that accelerates a swimmer's body forward." [2]

What could be more simple than envisioning your hand pushing backward?

Perhaps Maglischo believes the swimmer will naturally make the scull impulses required to find the still water. He may think that over describing a sculling component is more risky than under describing it, knowing that humans have the tendency to think "more is better."

If you identify with his description, just remember that Ernie says, "a predominantly backward direction..." He does not say "a completely backward direction...." You will be swimming like a stiff wooden paddle boat if you do not incorporate some intuitive impulsing.

I say that all of the above are correct. I also believe that envisioning a wall underneath you is correct if that engages your sense of FEEL with your hand and forearm.

Be careful not to picture the wall too low beneath you though, because that might cause you to drop the upper arm low in the water. Remember, the entire upper arm [our first lever] must be raised high. Our imaginary wall sits high in the water...perhaps only a foot below the surface.

The words that registered the most for me were "pressure on the water." This pressure is something you want to feel on every nook and cranny of your palm, fingers, and forearm. Every nook and cranny!

The wrist should be flush (straight) with the forearm so that you feel the pressure even in the crease between the forearm and palm. If you have a bend in the wrist, then you are missing an entire section of surface area where you should be feeling the water. Look at the photos on the following pages. Once the swimmer has caught the water and has a high elbow, the wrist is flush.

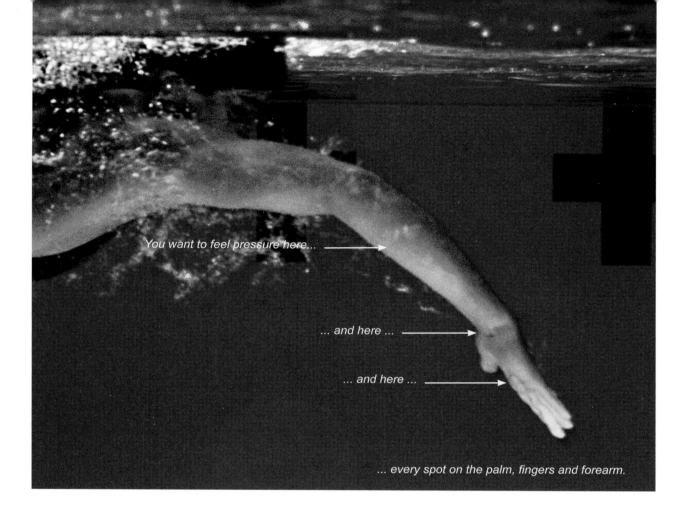

You want to feel pressure here...

... and here ...

... and here ...

... every spot on the palm, fingers and forearm.

Look at the picture above...it shows the places where you want to feel pressure

While it is no problem to point arrows directly to the mechanics of the high-elbow, pointing directly to "feel" is not so straight forward. However, look at the full pull sequences of the top swimmers on the following pages, and you will learn more about feel than words can describe or arrows can show.

While looking at the pull sequences, take note of the following:

1) The hand should be held with tone, but not rigid. Maximize surface area. Feel the water on every point of the palm and fingers. No cupping.

2) During the early phase of the pull, fin-

gertips point toward the bottom of the pool, but with no bend in the wrist. If you bend the wrist during the high-elbow phase, then you have lost the feel of the water in the crease where you forearm meets the palm. Also, by bending the wrist there is a much higher risk of dropping the elbow unknowingly, thinking you are doing the mechanics correctly because the fingers point downward. With a straight/flush wrist, the only way your fingertips will point to the bottom of the pool is if you employ the high-elbow position.

3) Count the number of sculls/impulses in these pull sequences. Once the swimmer has purchased the water in the high-elbow position, there are only two to three impulses.

4) Once the hand is anchored in the high-

elbow position, then the hips begin their drive in the other direction. The tractive force of the high-elbow position is required in order to rotate the hips.

5) Note the vertical search for still water rather than simply a lateral search. There is a diagonal component to the predominantly backward push.

Sheila Taormina, *Olympic Gold Medalist, World Champion*

*Mark Spitz enters the water and immediately bends his wrist, but then look at the frames that show the high-elbow…the wrist is straight/flush.

Mark Spitz, *1972 Olympic Gold Medalist. Photo courtesy: Indiana University, Counsilman Center for the Science of Swimming.*

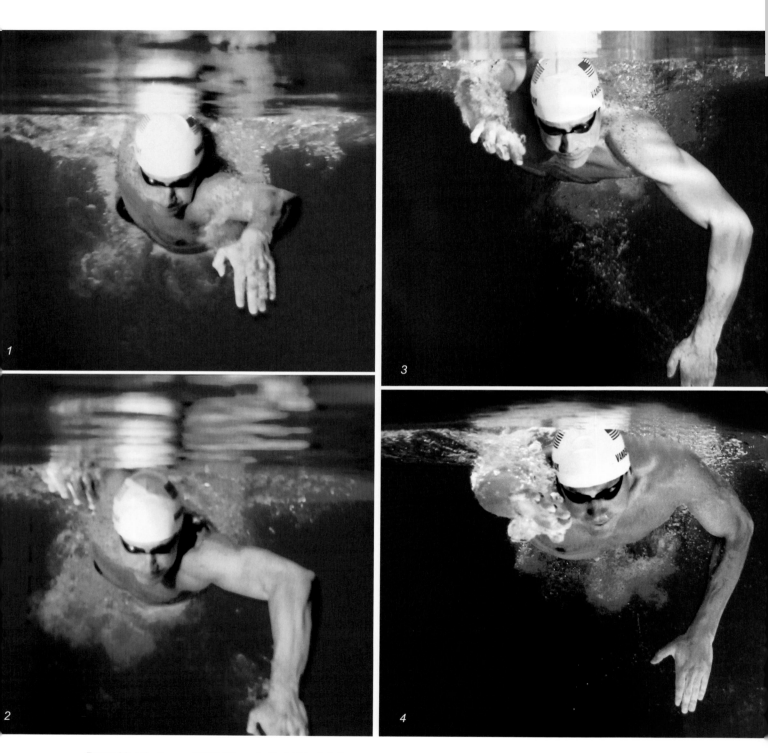

Peter Vanderkaay, *2008 Olympic Gold Medalist*

Allison Schmitt, 2008 Olympic Bronze Medalist

Why not pull with a straight arm?

A few of you may be asking why there has to be a bend in the elbow. Your reasoning may be, "If our goal is to hold the water, then it actually makes more sense to hold it with the entire arm as one long lever rather than only the forearm as a much shorter lever." Good instinct. There has indeed been a revolution in this direction, BUT... only in the world of sprinting!

The straight-arm freestyle requires a massive amount of power and strength that must specifically be developed in training. Sprinters who are attempting to develop this strength must be able to handle the extra resistive force that they get by holding more water.

Also keep in mind that a straighter arm is a longer arm, so it takes a longer path through the water. Anyone who attempts to apply more resistive force with the longer lever should check that their turnover rate is not negatively affected. Also, applying the extra force at such powerful turnover speeds is risky business (hello shoulder injury). If a swimmer chooses to go this route then he/she should understand every implication.

The straight-arm freestyle technique is not discussed in this book, because I am going to assume that most readers are either triathletes (competing in longer distances than the 50 and 100) or masters swimmers who are of the age, like I am (over 40), and who, like I, just pray that something doesn't snap. For age group swimmers (and some masters swimmers) who are sprinters, discuss with your coach whether or not you should work on a straight-arm pull.

Margaret Kelly, Seven-time NCAA All-American and Six-time Big Ten Champion, swimming with the straight-arm technique that she uses in the 50 and 100 freestyle.

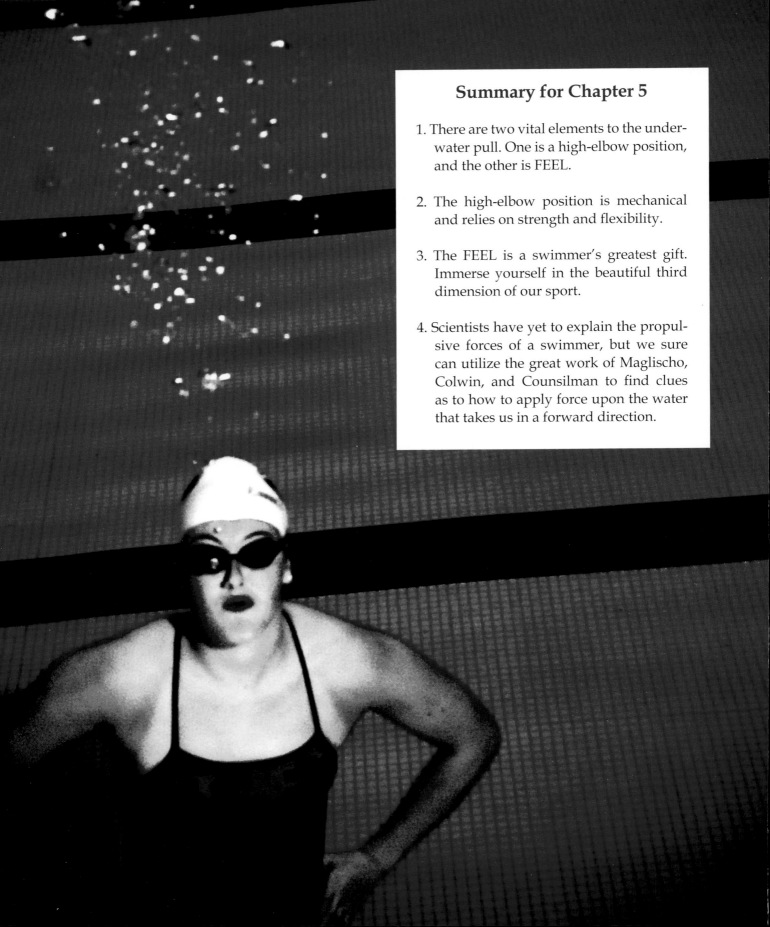

Summary for Chapter 5

1. There are two vital elements to the underwater pull. One is a high-elbow position, and the other is FEEL.

2. The high-elbow position is mechanical and relies on strength and flexibility.

3. The FEEL is a swimmer's greatest gift. Immerse yourself in the beautiful third dimension of our sport.

4. Scientists have yet to explain the propulsive forces of a swimmer, but we sure can utilize the great work of Maglischo, Colwin, and Counsilman to find clues as to how to apply force upon the water that takes us in a forward direction.

Chapter 6
Developing the Underwater Pull
strength, flexibility, and feel

Ok now - you have taken the path of least resistance for too long. I am going to toughen you up a whole lot, and you are going to love it! Soon you will be thanking me - perhaps not at first when your deltoids are on fire and your lats are so sore that you can barely lift your arms over your head - but soon after that you will be ecstatic that we crossed paths. You are going to come out the on the other end a true swimmer.

This chapter includes the drills and exercises which, if applied with focus and attention to technique, will develop both your high-elbow and feel for the water. If you are an adult who swims by yourself, then perfect. You will be able to fully concentrate on these exercises without interruption. For those of you who swim with a team, you may have to get creative with incorporating these exercises into the workouts. The best way I know for doing that is to communicate respectfully with your coach. I had a fantastic relationship with my coach, Greg, for 30 years - from age 9 until my final Olympic swim at age 39 - because we always shared ideas with each other (maybe not so much when I was 9, but you know what I mean....). Work as a team on figuring out a plan to incorporate these drills and exercises.

Slow down, you move too fast

Some of you will want to see a 5 second drop in your times on day one. Well, I am going to call you out on this. You are so focused on the product (your desired end result) that you have no time for considering the process (the elements that will actually take you to your desired end result). Switch your mode of thinking to a process-oriented mode. This is called "the journey," and it is the most lovely part of sport.

Performance results are fleeting anyway. I have an Olympic gold medal in my closet, yet today I will clean the kitty litter twice, do the dishes, throw in a load of laundry, and go to the mailbox where I will be greeted by a stack of bills just like all of you will. But…today, if I choose, I may go to the pool, dive in, and feel the water. I may engage my mind to take my body even a fraction closer to its full future potential. That is a great day in sport, in life.

Training the vital elements

The two vital elements (high-elbow and feel) may be trained in the same session. Even considering the mechanical nature of one element and the sensitive nature of the other, it is possible to work the high-elbow and the feel congruously. Some drills and exercises single out one element or the other, while other drills work both critical techniques at the same time.

The drills and exercises listed in this chapter address strength, flexibility, feel, or a combination. Let's start with ways we can train the more mechanical of the two vital elements -the high-elbow.

66

Developing the high-elbow

1) Flexibility and tone through streamlining: One of the most basic skills in competitive swimming is a streamlined push-off after the start and turns. The benefits are obvious: a reduced resistance that allows the swimmer to take advantage of the amazing propulsion generated by the legs from pushing off a solid starting block or pool wall (there is no doubt about Newton's Third Law when it comes to this). Why then do a significant number of age-group, masters, and collegiate swimmers not take streamlining 100% to heart? I think the reason is that many people take it for granted and believe it will be easy to do when race time comes. Not so. The flexibility required for a fabulous, effective streamline must be trained. It is an extremely strenuous position to develop.

Triathletes, you are not off the hook either. You may think it has nothing to do with you, since you contest your events in open water usually, but **streamlines are one of the most dynamic exercises for training muscle tone, explosiveness, and range of motion, including the flexibility required for a high elbow.** An athlete who passes up a streamline is passing up a free yoga workout off every wall.

Note in the photo to the left that the swimmer has hand on top of hand and is squeezing the elbows and biceps into the head, near the ears - squeezing as much as possible! This motion takes great strength and resiliency at first. It is not natural. The tissue in the shoulders, lats, and triceps is stiff, and it is actually painful to ask it to stretch so much. In addition to the squeezing of the arms against the head, the body/core is stretching as long as it possibly can stretch. The intercostal muscles, the abdominal muscles, the back, and the muscles that attach to the top of the pelvic bone must be elongated to the point of feeling 3 inches taller. If you stretch and squeeze this much, then, and only then, are you are doing a real streamline.

There are hidden benefits to this one simple (yet not so simple at first) exercise. First, you will gain the flexibility in the shoulder that helps you medially rotate your upper arm near your face/chin for the high-elbow position. The lats and back muscles will also gain flexibility, thus allowing you to jut forward from the scapula as you grab water out front during your pull.

The other benefit of streamlining brings me to a very important point about body position considerations in swimming. I made the statement earlier in the book that beach-goers who float on the surface of the water have as good a body position as I had at the Olympics. It is true. It is also true that almost every swimmer and triathlete I have seen has a body position this good too. The part that the beach-goers and most swimmers/triathletes are missing is **BODY TONE**. There is a big difference between body position and body tone.

I learned about body tone in my first year of equestrian show jumping. When I started riding at age 36, my coach was appalled at my posture and told me to "sit up." I tried to sit up, but it was exhausting. It was such a simple concept, yet I was unable to maintain it. He then explained that I should not be relaxed nor rigid. He used the word "tone." Bingo. It registered. Tone was what I had developed in swimming by doing hundreds of long streamlines each day. I had to take that same stretched-out strength and apply it to sitting up on the horse.

For you to be a strong athlete in any sport, you must have tone. In swimming. In running. In cycling. Hundreds of times each day you have opportunities to develop tone. Simply sitting up with good posture at your desk will strengthen the muscles of your core, front and back. Every push-off at swim practice is yet another level for developing this. When you run and feel fatigued, take note of your core posture. Are you hunching over? Or are you elongating and maintaining a composed posture? It is good to push yourself to longer and longer distances in training, whether it is in swimming, running, or other endurance activities, but if you lose your posture and tone, then you are weakening, not strengthening.

Please, if you have energy to choose only one thing from this entire book, choose this first exercise of streamlining. It is so simple, yet so neglected for lack of understanding of all its benefits. Place it at the top of your list, and focus every time you push off the wall. Your tissue will respond beautifully within a week or two of consistent effort.

2) Tubing and Halo Bench: Taking it up a notch, if you want to make the most dramatic gains in both the flexibility and strength required for a high elbow, then that is best accomplished out of the water. Developing "feel" is different; you have no choice but to be in the water for that. But, for the high-elbow you are actually at risk of being way off the mark if you only work on in-water drills, for the reason that water throws us off our rockers. Our perceptions of what we think we are doing in the water are often not even close to what we are actually doing.

The most logical place for working on strength outside of the water is in the weight room, but unfortunately there are no machines that fully simulate the high-elbow position in swimming. We can train the deltoids, triceps and lats with various exercises but not in the way we actually pull. On top of that, when we lift weights we rarely work at a tempo pace. The Halo Bench and tubing was specifically designed to train a swimmer's high-elbow position and TEMPO (rate of turnover that we discussed in Chapter 2).

To clarify… I am a proponent of weight lifting and general strength for swimming (and cycling/running/triathlon too). My advice is to do a strength program, and to make tubing training a part of it.

Look at the photos on the right and note the similarities between the position of the the arm/hand training on the Halo with the underwater photo of the high-elbow.

You may also use the tubing alone, without the Halo bench. It requires that you regularly check to ensure proper technique, since the Halo template is not present. If you are cognizant of this technique, then the physical benefits of the tubing-only set up are equal to that of the Halo bench set up.

CAUTION! The Halo Bench and tubing simulate only the **underwater** portion of the swim stroke. Do not recover your arm over your head as you would do while swimming. The tension on the tubing is too much for the shoulder. The correct technique for recovering the arm back to the starting position is to take the same, yet reversed direction, path on the recovery that you took when pulling back.

How do you know if you are doing the tubing exercise correctly or not? The first clue is that your fingertips point toward the ground at the beginning of the pull. You must do this without bending your wrist. If you bend at the wrist, then you are able to achieve downward-pointing fingertips with a low elbow. Not good. You will be no closer to developing the high-elbow VITAL ELEMENT if you do this.

Keep the wrist straight and flush with the forearm throughout the entire front phase of the stroke. Should the wrist have tone? You bet. Think of your wrist as not relaxed, not rigid - but with tone.

The other key to proper technique when doing the tubing is to keep the upper arm raised. Do not allow that lever to drop at a downward angle. One way to think about it is to keep the upper arm parallel with the ground. Another way to picture it is to keep your elbow the same height as your shoulder (the purpose of the Halo template is to ensure this aspect.) It will also be obvious that you are doing this correctly if your deltoid muscle burns so badly that you are ready to cry "Uncle!"

Lastly, when concentrating on your technique with the tubing be sure to finish near your hip rather than wide and out. Look at the photo of the underwater stroke on the next page, and take particular note of where the hand is finishing. It is brushing the hip just as the photo to the right depicts with the tubing.

When I opened this chapter by saying you were going to toughen up and no longer take

the path of least resistance, the tubing training is exactly what I had in mind. These exercises will fire up your deltoids in 10-15 seconds, and your lats will be incredibly sore the next day. This is good though! The shaking in the muscles you are going to feel from tubing exercises will make you stronger. Too often we avoid pain because we associate it with "bad." A simple adjustment in perspective will help you endure the short amount of time you will feel the burning from the following sets. Stay strong. Stick with it. You will feel great within a couple of weeks.

The workouts on the following pages may be done with the Halo Bench or with the tubing alone. These are just suggestions. Feel free to adjust or make up your own sets. The only thing that is imperative is that you concentrate fully on technique.

Note: Tubing is easily hooked onto any anchored pole at a pool, such as diving boards, ladders, backstroke flag poles, etc.

A quick note to new swimmers: Chapter 3 ended with a paragraph addressing new swimmers who may need to work at first on becoming comfortable with the water but who could still make great strides on the pull doing dry-land exercises. This section on tubing and the Halo Bench is the section to which I was referring. These exercises are intended as much for you as they are for the swimmer who has competed for decades.

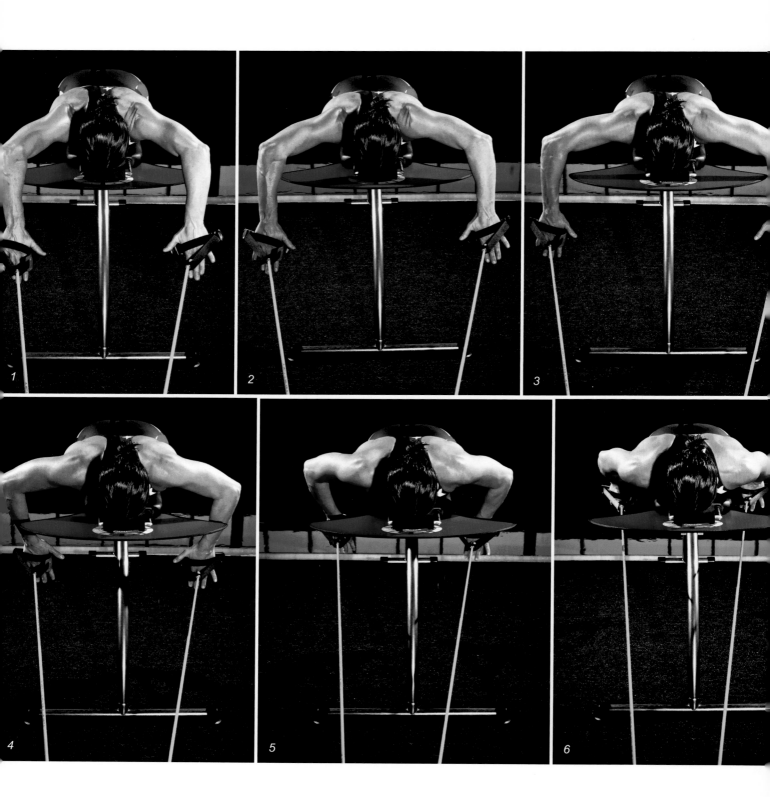

A full pull sequence on the Halo Bench

IMPROPER TECHNIQUE Example 1: *The two photos above show a dropped elbow and a bent wrist. It is important that you check that your elbow is high and your wrist is straight/flush before pulling back.*

IMPROPER TECHNIQUE Example 2: *In the photos above, the wrist is straight but the entire first lever (upper arm) has been dropped. It is important that you check the height of your elbow before pulling back.*

Training sets with the Halo Bench and tubing

Weeks 1-2: Do the following three days per week. Technique is everything. Start with your arm in the high-elbow position. STOP! Hold it there. Check everything before pulling back *slowly* (we are not working on tempo at this point). Check the following:

1. Your fingertips point downward.
2. Your wrist is straight/flush with your forearm.
3. Your upper arm is parallel with the ground (or check that your elbow is the same height as your shoulder).

Ensure these three technique points before EVERY PULL back.

Remember to recover back to the starting position with your hand/arm low, taking the reverse path you took on the pull. Do not recover as you would if you were swimming in the water.

Do 3 x 8 pulls back with each arm (6 sets of 8 total), finishing all the way back to brush your hip. You may alternate arms or do a full set of 8 with one arm, take a rest, and then switch arms. Take as much rest as necessary between sets (1 minute is recommended). If you cannot do a full 8 to start, that is fine. You will still make progress even if you only do 5 per set. The key is to go slowly and ensure technique.

Weeks 3-4: Do the following 3 days per week. Technique is still the most important factor (it always will be). Now you should be starting to feel more comfortable with the position. Everything is the same as Weeks 1-2, but now try 3 x 12 repeats with each arm. Be sure to check your position before pulling back.

Try to go out of your comfort zone just a bit by feeling the tissue of the upper lat (that attaches into your armpit area) extend. You will be jutting the scapula more and trying to medially rotate your shoulder near your face/ chin. Small gains in range of motion make a big difference in athletic performance, so push just slightly out of your natural range.

Weeks 5 and beyond: Now you know whether or not you are ready for more or need to stick with a concentrated slow technique. Either is fine. Below are suggestions and tips for progressing. Just promise me one thing - that you will never sacrifice proper technique for a hammerhead mentality. OK? Thank you.

a) Train in time increments rather than a set number of repeats. Do sets of 30 seconds, 45 seconds, or 1 minute. Build up the number of sets you do. Start with three sets and increase to 6 sets as the weeks progress.

You may do two arms at a time or stay with alternating one-arm freestyle rhythm. The butterfly pull pattern is the same as freestyle when doing tubing. The upper body workout is the same, but your core will feel a slightly dif-ferent training effect between the butterfly two-arm and the freestyle one-arm. I like to alternate sets, half being butterfly and half freestyle.

Note: When I was swimming before 1996 I pulled on the tubing 4 days per week for 14-15 minutes total pulling time each day. The sets varied from 3 x 5 minutes to 7 x 2 minutes. I simulated my 200 Meter Freestyle goal for tempo and number of strokes when I did 2 minute repeats. I did this after my evening swim practice, and rested for two minutes between sets. This is quite a bit of tubing exercise. It is not necessary to do this much.

As a triathlete I incorporated tubing 3 days per week and only did 7-8 minutes pulling time each day. Sets varied from 7 x 1 minute, to 4 x 2 minutes, to 5 x 1:30 with a rest period equal to pulling time.

b) Incorporate tubing into your swim workout. Once a week you should plan a swimming set within your overall workout in which you alternate a swim repeat with a tubing repeat. For instance, choose 6 x 100 freestyle, and after each 100 freestyle press out of the water and do either a :15, :30, :45, or 1:00 pull on tubing, depending on your level of strength. Take approximately 15 seconds rest before diving in (or pushing off the wall) for the next 100. The goal for your 100 freestyle swim is to keep great form. You will be fatigued in the deltoids, lats and triceps. Maintain your composure and tone. You may do the 100s for form only, or you may decide to include a fast 25 at some point as a challenge.

c) Add in an exercise that isolates the triceps. This is for variety and additional strength. Example: If you do a 30-second repeat on the tubing, add a short spurt of tricep isolation at the end, for approximately 10-20 seconds. The tricep isolation is simply the back finish of your stroke. It burns tremendously but has great benefits. This is a very short, quick motion.

Look at the photos to the right to understand the short range of motion in this exercise. Also, take note that the fingertips are always pointing downward, and that your wrist must flex (with tone) during the back push of the stroke.

Tubing is easily attached to any anchored pole at the pool.

d) Train your tempo for a specific race. As mentioned already, I trained my 200 Freestyle strategy (tempo) out of the water with tubing almost as much as I did in the water. You should know your goal tempo. If you do not, then work with your coach on this. If you swim alone then ask a friend to go to the pool with you and time your rate. Training turnover rate/tempo on tubing is ideal. The next chapter explains and reviews the top swimmer's tempos.

One final note: Tubing is a great training tool that you can pack in a suitcase easily and do in a hotel room if you travel, simply by attaching it to a door handle in your room.

The short range of motion of the tricep isolation exercise is depicted above.

3) Press-outs: There is one thing in life that simulates the high-elbow position: pressing up and over walls. Although most likely not part of your daily routine, you have a chance to train this movement simply by pressing up and out of the pool. The photos to the right show the exercise. Notice if you take the vertical position of the press-out and transfer it to a horizontal plane, it is the same position as the high-elbow we want to develop in our swimming.

You should incorporate sets of press-outs into your training. Do 3 x 10 after a workout, or make up a set similar to the alternating swim/tubing set described earlier: 6 x 100 freestyle, but this time do 5 -10 press-outs after each 100 free. Take 15 seconds rest before pushing off for the next 100.

A set my coach had me do regularly was 10 x 50, pressing out after each repeat and diving in for the next 50. The interval was always tight, usually :40. I had to swim the 50 in approximately :30, which would give just enough time to press out, stand up, turn around, take a few breaths, and dive in for the next 50. By the end of 10 it is not so easy.

To conclude this section: If you incorporate streamlines, Halo/tubing, and press outs into your training routine you will be as strong as Tarzan, capable of wrestling alligators and all that good stuff. But you are not ready to swim fast on that alone; you still need FEEL.

When doing press-outs, place your hands slightly wider than your shoulders

Developing the "Feel"

As mentioned earlier, we must be in the water to develop a "feel" for it. There are no dry-land exercises that simulate the sensation of resistive forces against a fluid. In order to understand the very element that mystifies us, we had better jump in and become friends with it. The following pages describe five in-water drills that develop the "feel."

1) Sculling: Sculling is the most important drill for learning "feel." The best way to convey its importance is to tell a true story:

In 1996, at our Olympic team training camp in Knoxville, Tennessee, one week before the opening of the Games, I was doing a 5,000 meter workout with a few of the women on the team. Other teammates were in their lanes churning out workouts, but Gary Hall Jr., our top sprinter on the team, was standing on the deck in the sun. After soaking in the rays for a while he decided to slip into the water in the lane next to me.

I was repeating 100s, and every time I came to the wall there was Gary, standing in the water chest high, never getting one hair on his head wet, sculling his hands back and forth in the water slowly and with great concentration. After 10 minutes he got out of the pool, and I heard him say to the coaches, "Ok, I've got my feel for the water. See you later."

Gary won two gold and two silver medals at those Olympics, and he went on to make two more Olympic teams in 2000 and 2004, winning gold in the 50 Meter Freestyle both times.

His entire workout that day was a sculling workout. He never went horizontal for a moment. I am not saying that all of us should do only sculling workouts from now on. First of all, Gary was tapering. Secondly, Gary is a sprinter, and often sprinters are a different breed. Gary even falls into the category of being a different breed from the different breed (incredible talent and awareness). While I do not know how much he trained in terms of aerobic sets, endurance, sprinting, and weights, I do know that he did not get away with only sculling every workout, nor can the rest of us. However, we can at least deduce from this story that FEEL is critical and that sculling is a fantastic tool for training the feel.

Now let's move on and describe the sculling motion and how to train it. There are many options. It is not necessary that you get your hair wet. You can stand chest high in the water like Gary did and scull in a vertical position (this is perfect for beginners), but I recommend sculling while lying horizontally, as in the swimming position. This way you are able to work the high-elbow position while feeling the water. Look at the photos on the next page to learn the sculling pattern.

The key is to feel pressure on every part of the hand and forearm, even the crease in the wrist. I will remind you again - do not bend the wrist. Hold your hands with tone.

Think about every point on the thumb. Are you feeling pressure on every spot?

Do the same with the pinky. Do you feel pressure on that?

Switch your attention to the crease in your wrist where your forearm meets the palm of your hand. You should feel pressure there too. Everywhere. Move your attention to your forearm and make sure you feel the water along the entire lever.

Look closely at the sculling photos and take note that the upper arm does not move. The sculling motion is taking place 100% with the forearm and hands, sweeping out and then sweeping back in.

The palms are turned outward at a 45 degree angle on the out-sweep, and then inward at the same angle on the in-sweep.

Never straighten the elbow during the sculling/sweeping motion. Always keep the high-elbow position throughout the entire exercise. Keep everything in front of you, perhaps just slightly wider than shoulder width.

Lastly, resist the urge to pull back; we are not working Newton's Third Law here. Instead, we are working small impulses and sculls that

allow us to understand how to search for still water when we apply everything to our swimming stroke.

You may kick lightly while you scull, for coordination purposes. Do not kick so much that it propels you forward significantly. Your face should be in the water, lifting forward (not to the side) for a breath. Watch your hands and forearm, ensuring a high elbow, but mostly concentrate on your feel. You may do sculling with a snorkel so that you do not have to lift your head for a breath.

Do 6 -10 times 25 yards (or meters) of sculling, three times per week, and you will be on your way to understanding the most glorious gift of swimming.

2) High-elbow, relaxed, out-of-water-recovery and hand-entry drill: This is not a drill as much as it is normal swimming with a specific concentration (let's call it a drill anyway).

First, I should clarify that the term "high-elbow" is going to be used as part of the description of this drill, but it is not referring to the same "high-elbow" we have been learning thus far. In swimming, there are two times during the full stroke cycle when a coach will refer to a "high-elbow." One of them is vital, and you know all about it already - it happens under the water. The other, which we are about to discuss, is not vital, but it is highly recommended for setting up the vital aspects of the pull. It happens above the water, during the recovery phase of the stroke.

The purpose of this drill is to set up the entry of the hand into the water correctly. Many swimmers erroneously believe that reaching far out in front of their head and entering the water with the arm almost fully extended lends to a longer distance per stroke. It does not. Distance per stroke is determined by how far the body moves, not how far the hand reaches. Not only does a far reach on the recovery not provide benefit, but more often than not it actually causes problems, including the body going off balance, poor rhythm/timing of the stroke, a pressing down motion of the arm once in the water, and worst of all a complete lack of feel at the most critical moment of the stroke...the entry.

I will not go into every detail of each problem just listed above, because I have a feeling that you understand swimming more now than ever and can probably answer the questions for yourself, but I do want to elaborate on the last one - the lack of feel at the critical moment of the stroke. Let's go back to Cecil Colwin's theory of propulsion, in which he describes vortices and the concept of shaping the flow of water.

Part of Colwin's advice to swimmers is to feel for the "oncoming flow" of water during the hand entry phase of the stroke. If you watch the top swimmers, especially those who have longer strokes out front (NOT gliding strokes, but full-arm extensions), these swimmers enter their hand into the water just in front of their head (12-18 inches), and then, as the hand/arm extends, the entire second lever (forearm and hand) is FEELING the water flow. These swimmers are, in a sense, becoming friends with the water, engaging in a relationship, as they extend. Once they are at full extension they smoothly maintain that relationship and roll into their high-elbow underwater position.

Look at video or still pictures of the top swimmers as they extend in the water before going into the high-elbow. While it is easier to see the swimmer's search for "feel" during the in-water extension on slow motion video, even the still photos show it, if you look carefully. There is a great sensitivity, that can actually be seen.

A swimmer who tries to reach out long in front before entering the hand/arm into the water misses the chance to feel the flow of water. They have missed out on sensitivity that will be vital once the underwater propulsion phase begins.

The drill I am finally getting around to describing to you now is, as I mentioned, more of a concentrated swimming exercise. The purpose is to develop a hand/arm entry that is sensitive to the flow of water so that you get into your high-elbow position under the water with great FEEL. So, swim normally - but SLOWLY - and once your hand in back finishes near your hip, begin the out-of-water recovery with a relaxed arm. Lead with the elbow.

*Look at the sensitivity in **Allison Schmitt**'s hand and fingers as she extends in the water. Once she has reached full extension she maintains her feel for the water as she moves into the high-elbow position.*

Your elbow should lift as if you were a puppet being directed by a puppeteer. Only lift the elbow; your forearm should dangle, relaxed. In fact, on this swimming drill, shake-out your hand and fingers as you recover. That is how relaxed you should be.

Once your forearm/hand recovers, enter your hand into the water 12-18 inches in front of your head. Allow the hand to "slip" into the water. From this point, concentrate on the sensitivity of the water on your hand and forearm. You may go to full extension, or you may begin the high-elbow underwater before you get to full extension. This will be a function of your personal style and strength.

This drill is similar to the "zipper" drill and "fingertip drag" drill you may know. Those two drills are equally acceptable to do as a replacement for this slow concentrated swimming, but make sure that part of why you do those two drills is to gain a sensitivity of the water that will flow into the high-elbow hold.

I encourage you to do this every day, 10 x 25 yards/meters, or more if you are someone who has over-reached for years.

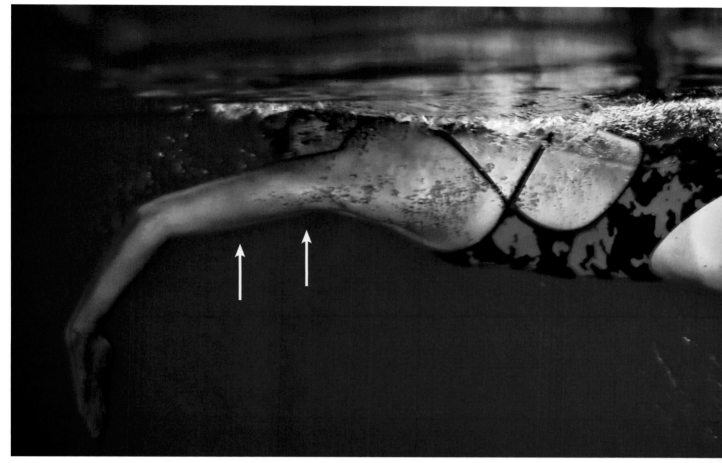

The water can act as a bed, aiding your high-elbow position.

One other really neat thing to try to feel when doing this drill is the flow of water under your first lever (your upper arm – from your shoulder to elbow). Remember that we want to keep this lever high in the water. If you concentrate enough, you will actually feel the water acting as a bed, aiding in holding up your upper arm. You should feel it in the arm-pit area too. That is the underside of the upper lever, right? Utilize the water to hold up that entire underside part of your upper arm.

One last note before moving on to the next drill: since the out-of-water recovery is not a vital element of the swim stroke, you are at liberty to do whatever you want to do with it really. If it does not negatively impact the vital elements, then design it any which-way you desire. The most well-known example of a stroke that incorporated a non-textbook recovery and entry was the windmill stroke of Janet Evans. Janet is arguably the best distance swimmer in all of history, and she had an extremely unorthodox stroke above the water in which she wind-milled with a straight arm. The key is that her straight-arm recovery and entry did not affect her ability to get a hold of the water. She was able to find a sensitivity quickly upon entering, and then apply it to the high-elbow position under the water immediately. If you are able to do this too, then it is perfectly acceptable.

3) Catch-up drill: Most of us know this drill. It is the one where we essentially swim normal freestyle except that the hand out front is waiting for the other hand to recover over the water and touch it before starting the pull: I almost did not include this drill in the book, because it leads many people to think that the top swimmers really do some sort of catch-up with their strokes and that this drill, with its emphasis on waiting out front, is training a glide and wait phase. This type of thinking could not be more off the mark.

Top swimmers do not glide. In fact, the phrase **"front-quadrant swimming" has been fully misinterpreted by the masses as gliding out front.** The hand that is out front, ready to pull, is not waiting for the other hand to come around. The true swimmer is working with tremendous sensitivity and strength to feel for the purchase of the water and begin the high-elbow position. This is the most dynamic, im-

portant part of the swim stroke, thus the last thing a swimmer should do at this stage is be engaged in such a passive activity as gliding.

Look at the photo of Peter Vanderkaay to the right. His right hand has just entered the water, and the pulling arm (left arm) is already significantly into the propulsive phase of the stroke. It makes no sense for Peter to glide with one hand out front while the other is recovering. Which hand at this moment is providing forward propulsion? Neither. This is not a good thing. By gliding, not only is momentum lost, but also the rate of turnover slows dramatically, having an overall negative effect on our equation from Chapter 2.

The truth behind front-quadrant swimming is that both hands are indeed in the front quadrant of the stroke length. They are both in front of, or near, the head, but the pulling hand has already done a huge amount of work

Allison Schmitt, 2008 Olympian, demonstrates the catch-up drill.

Peter Vanderkaay *has one of the longest stroke rates among Olympic swimmers (1.6 seconds per full stroke cycle...see next chapter for details); yet, even with his long stroke his pulling hand never remained extended - gliding - waiting for the recovering arm to enter the water.*

to grab the water, get into the high-elbow position, AND pull the body forward to the point that it is about to pass over the pulling hand. All of this has taken place before the entry hand has even come close to extending. The pulling hand NEVER stayed in a glide position waiting for the other hand.

The concept of "extension" has been misconstrued as "gliding," and I believe the lack of understanding of hip roll is the culprit. The reality of the underwater scene is that a truly effective hip roll accentuates an acceleration of the finishing hand while providing natural extension to the hand that is initiating the catch. Top swimmers NEVER remain static on the rotated hip, gliding. Once the hips drive to one side, the swimmer immediately switches direction to accentuate the drive to the other side. The drive and change of direction is only possible when the pulling hand has traction on the water.

Going back to the catch-up drill, the real benefit is that the swimmer has time to pause and concentrate on the underwater pull, one arm at a time. When the finishing hand has recovered and touched the other hand, the primary focus is then placed on establishing the high-elbow position with the pulling arm. Attention may also be placed on the feel for the water and application of pressure as the swimmer pulls his/her body forward.

One strange feeling you should expect while doing the catch-up drill is the feeling of lost momentum. Since there are phases when neither hand is propelling, we must re-start the momentum on each pull. It will never feel as fluid as when we actually swim the normal stroke with a rhythmic tempo pace. Do not rush the learning process though. Accept that it takes time to develop a high elbow and feel before we can build tempo into the equation.

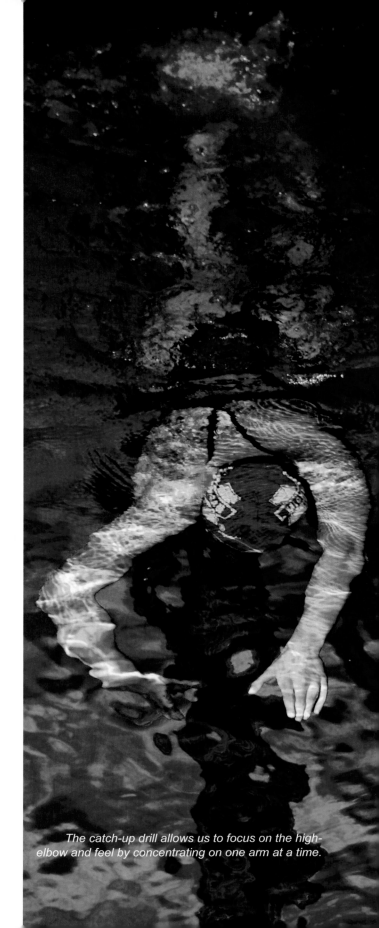

The catch-up drill allows us to focus on the high-elbow and feel by concentrating on one arm at a time.

4) One arm drill: The purpose of this drill is exactly the same as the catch-up drill - concentrating on one arm at a time so that you may work the high-elbow and feel without worrying about the timing of the full stroke. You may do this drill with the non-pulling arm at your side or out in front of you.

Do a full 25 yards/meters with one arm, and then switch arms on the next length. Just as with the catch-up drill you should expect that there will be a feeling of lost momentum. The important thing to remember is that this is to be done slowly, with concentration and sensitivity for feel.

Allison Schmitt demonstrating the one-arm drill with her non-pulling arm at her side.

5) One arm pull with kick-board drill: I first saw this drill taught in 1999 by a man named Doug Stern. Even though I was 30 years old and had been swimming for 25 years, this drill immediately became my favorite. In addition to developing a feel for the water, it builds strength everywhere.

How to do it: You will need a kick-board for this drill. Place one hand in the middle of the kick-board. With your head above water, and with your legs kicking moderately, stroke with your free hand. The focus is placed first and foremost on the high-elbow position underwater (we are no longer working on the high-elbow recovery out of the water with this drill). Watch your fingertips as your hand enters the water. Are they pointing down? Are they pointing down with a straight/flush wrist? Is your upper arm high in the water? The answer to all of these questions should be "yes."

Do 25 yards/meters stroking with one arm; rest at the wall for approximately 15 seconds (you will be tired); then switch arms for the next 25. Do 12 x 25 total (6 x 25 each arm) three days per week.

The real benefits start to show when you are able to build in the "feel" for the water while you do this. You will know if you are doing it correctly if the kick-board surges on each pull. Try to see how much of a surge you can build into the stroke as you keep the high-elbow position. Your core will build tone on this drill too, because the arm that is placed on the kick-board does a fair amount of work to stabilize the body.

A wrap

That wraps it up. The 3 exercises listed for high-elbow development, and the 5 drills listed for the "feel," will keep you busy. You choose which work best for you. I do them for strength, range of motion, and the enjoyment of feeling the water still today, even though I have retired from competition. Even if I was training and competing still, I would incorporate these exercises and drills into my workouts.

Should you only do drills? What about regular swimming?

You will go nuts if you do drills 100% of the time for the next three months. I recommend regular freestyle swimming (and other strokes, kicking, pulling, etc.) not only so that you keep your sanity, but also for a training effect. Drills, drills, nothing but drills, will make you one of the most uncoordinated people on the planet. You will forget what you set out to do in the first place. Just remember to THINK during every lap. Do not "check out" mentally and revert to old muscle memory. Constantly focus on developing your new muscle memory.

While swimming, be conscious of whether or not you are dropping your elbow...even take a peek at it now and then. Look to see that your fingertips are pointing toward the bottom of the pool during the early phase of the underwater pull; also look to see that the wrist is straight/flush during this phase. Then switch your attention to a sensitivity of feel, pressure, resistive forces and traction - think about every point on your palm, wrist, forearm, and even the space between your fingers.

If the fingers are held properly (together but not tightly) then there is a webbing-like effect, and you will feel the traction even on the sides of each finger. Think about the tissue of your shoulder medially rotating into your neck/chin area more. Push yourself to gain that flexibility even while you are swimming normally. Do the same with the muscles in your lats/scapula/back.

It will most definitely feel awkward, mechanical, and uncomfortable at first, but it is worth the journey. Soon enough you will be flowing into the position as if your body was originally designed for this range of motion.

Oh, and ALWAYS do a streamline off every wall!

Wait, let me clarify: Do a great streamline off every wall!

A tip for all swimmers...but especially for age-group, high school, and collegiate swimmers

When you feel fatigue in practice, especially during the all-out swims, this is the most important time to maintain a high elbow and traction on the water. Do not allow your elbow to drop due to fatigue. Stay composed; focus on technique. Not only does this do wonders for your physical strength and muscle memory (because this is when the "training effect" sets in), but also it is what puts the meaning back into the mental side of sport. It is called mental toughness and focus.

"Focus" means "thinking about the things that are within your control." Technique is always in your control.

Learn how to focus regularly in practice. Your times may just drop to levels you never knew you had in you.

Summary for Chapter 6

TONE . . . focus . . . . STREAMLINE . . . . the process . . . . THE JOURNEY . . .

fingertips point downward . . . . FLUSH WRIST . . . . posture . . . . TECHNIQUE . . .

fatigue = opportunity to become stronger . . . . COMPOSURE . . .

TONE . . . focus . . . . STREAMLINE . . . . the process . . . . THE JOURNEY . . . .

fingertips point downward . . . FLUSH WRIST . . . . posture . . . . TECHNIQUE . . .

fatigue = opportunity to become stronger . . . . COMPOSURE

Chapter 7
Our Equation from Chapter 2 Applied
stroke counts and rates of top swimmers

The previous chapter focused on developing the technique of the underwater pull, and it stressed the need to slow down and concentrate while learning the new muscle memory. This is extremely important; swimming is first and foremost about technique. Without technique, strength and conditioning mean very little. Eventually, however, if we want to be fast, then power and speed must be built in to the stroke. This chapter explains what that entails.

The equation (# Strokes) x (Rate) = TIME is our guiding star. Thinking back to the two examples in Chapter 2, you should now have an entirely new appreciation for this equation. To refresh your memory, we singled out the "long glider" whose turnover rate was disastrously slow, and then we looked at the enthusiastic 8 & Under who spun wildly and took a record-breaking number of strokes to get across the pool.

The specific numbers I plugged into the equation in Chapter 2 were simply examples. In this chapter we are going to look at the real numbers. Most importantly I want to tie everything we have learned about propulsion and the underwater pull together with our guiding-star equation.

What are the real numbers?

There are two factors in the equation we need to review: # Strokes and Rate. The underwater pull affects both dramatically. Let's jump right in and look at the numbers.

The stroke rates of top swimmers are consistently in the range between **1.15 seconds per full stroke cycle to 1.6 seconds per full stroke cycle**. Sprinters (50 and 100 meter specialists) typically have a faster rate, sometimes even under 1 second per full cycle, but usually between 1.0 and 1.2.

Do these numbers sound quick? They should, because they are. You might be asking yourself, "Does this mean that even the big guys are only taking one and a half seconds per full arm cycle through the water? It looks so much longer and slower than that." Well, it is indeed just as you are wondering. Even the swimmers who extend the most (Ian Thorpe of Australia [the Thorpedo], Michael Phelps, and many other top men) have rates of only 1.5-1.6 seconds per full arm cycle.

Remember, when we talk about rate of turnover we are counting full stroke cycles (from the time the right arm enters the water until it enters again, or left arm to left arm).

The stroke rate numbers prove that top swimmers do not glide. There simply is no time for them to remain out in front, gliding twice (remember, each arm is part of the full cycle) and still make it around in one and a half seconds. And we are talking about the LONGEST stroke rates right now. The most common rates are even faster - 1.3 to 1.4 seconds per cycle.

So, you may want to know what they are doing? You already know the answer. They are getting into the high-elbow position so as to be able to **hold** the water and do what a real swimmer does: pull the body over the arm that has just "purchased" the water. This is how elite swimmers get distance per stroke. Even the swimmers who fully extend their arm are feeling the sensitivity of the water the entire time so that they may get into their high-elbow position and start the propulsion phase of the stroke immediately after extension.

Once the swimmer is in a high-elbow position, then the path the hand takes does not sweep wide and far to find still water. It is predominantly a backward path (remember, we need to move FORWARD) with impulses/sculls and diagonal pushes to find still water.

Remember, the hand searches for still water along a vertical spectrum. Look again at the full pull sequences of the top swimmers in Chapter 5 and you will see this. The top swimmers do not simply scull outward or inward, but they also take advantage of the third dimension and find still water perhaps just a bit higher or lower in the water at various phases of the pull. At no point however are they searching very far away.

Just as a long glide out front kills our turnover rate, so does a long and meandering path under the water. Your pull pattern must find still water in order to maintain resistance that moves you forward, but you need not launch a full-fledged search expedition to find it.

Look closely at the photos in this book over and over. You will learn more by studying those than anything I could write in words.

Different strokes for different folks

Why do some top swimmers have a 1.1 rate and others a 1.6 rate?

As mentioned at the beginning of Chapter 5, some top swimmers get into the high-elbow position almost immediately when their hand enters the water in front of their head. Their strokes appear choppy and short, almost crab-like. They do not extend to a full straight arm. These swimmer's rates are often in the range of 1.1 to 1.2. They will take more strokes than other swimmers, but their rate is considerably quicker. They are optimizing the two numbers in the equation in a manner that suits their strength, flexibility and personal attributes best.

These quick turnovers and shorter stroke lengths are most commonly seen in female distance swimmers. While the equation for these swimmers is optimized in many ways, the shortcoming is that such a stroke does not support the really high gears of swimming speed. When they are entered in a shorter event that requires more speed (the 50, 100, and 200), it is often difficult for many of them to effectively employ a more powerful stroke. This does not matter so much, however, since their forte' is distance swimming (400 and above).

The example above is not meant to imply that all female distance swimmers stroke with quick turnovers and shorter pulls. The intent of the example is to show that it is one option for balancing the equation. It works for a certain percentage of top swimmers. I do believe, however, that there is a shift away from this in women's distance swimming, as strength training is more and more a part of every swimmer's program now. Distance swimming is not solely about tempo and endurance any longer; it appears that strength and power are coming into the equation now. The stroke rate and stroke count numbers included at the end of this chapter show the slight trend.

Going back to our review of "different strokes for different folks," in order to have the *most* power output, a swimmer must have a longer stroke length *and* the capability of turning over quickly. Sprinters are the perfect example of maximizing the equation in this way. They employ a powerful stroke that gets distance from each pull and has a fast turnover (1.0-1.1). The obvious limitations in this are in maintaining the power and speed over a longer distance; therefore, just as a distance swimmer has difficulty switching to a more powerful gear, many sprinters are at a loss to find a gear that works for longer races.

Both groups have a feel for the water and high elbows (except sprinters who train the straight-arm technique). It is the manner in which they apply force and speed to the pull that determines whether they are more suited as a distance specialist or a sprinter.

Middle-distance swimmers are no different; they also rely on the vital elements of a high elbow and feel while optimizing the balance of stroke count and stroke rate for their event. Since some middle-distance swimmers are sprint oriented while others are distance oriented, the range of numbers in stroke rate and stroke count among this group varies. Some will tend toward a longer, more powerful stroke with a slower turnover (1.5-1.6), while others swim with a shorter stroke length and faster turnover (1.2-1.4).

The most strategic middle distance race is the 200. Not only will you see a wide range of turnover rates among swimmers in a pool, but also you will see a single swimmer changing his/her rate within the 200. A 200 swimmer will often employ a longer, more powerful stroke during the first 100 of a 200, with a rate 1.4-1.6, and then will pick up the tempo on the last 100, or the last 50, and stroke at a rate 1/10 of a second faster or more per full stroke cycle. This is part of a strategy that the swimmer and coach design to maximize the equation at various points of such a strategic race.

The bottom line is that there are no rules. The general range is 1.0-1.6, and this covers just about every top swimmer in the spectrum. **The top athletes are optimizing the equation in a way that best suits them and their event.** The key is that they are aware that the equation needs to be optimized.

What are the masses doing?

I see the masses still focused on one thing: reducing resistance through body position, gliding, and over-reaching. The rates of triathletes and masters swimmers are almost always over 2.0 seconds per full stroke cycle, and they go so high as 3.0. You can now see that even the longest Olympic stroke rates (1.5-1.6) are significantly faster than the rates of swimmers who focus on gliding.

The high-elbow position and feel are the key to Distance Per Stroke (taking fewer strokes) while not sacrificing rate of turnover. Athletes who glide out front may be able to take as few strokes as the top swimmers, but they are virtually twice as slow due to rate of turnover.

How to take your rate

Since it is impossible for you to swim and operate a stop watch at the same time, you will have to ask a coach or a friend to take your rate for you. Explain to them that it does not matter which arm they time. The key is that they start the watch when your arm enters the water, and then stop it when that same arm has completed a full cycle and enters the water again. They should take it multiple times throughout a 100 yard/meter swim. They should also occasionally time two full cycles and then divide the number in half. This minimizes minor errors in their timing.

How to count your strokes

Counting strokes is not difficult, but it does require concentration. You can count your own strokes, but it is not a bad idea to have a coach or friend count them for you as well. It does not matter if you are in a 25 yard pool, a 25 meter pool, or a 50 meter pool for counting, but you will only be able to make comparisons between your stroke count and the stroke counts of others if you are comparing from a same length pool. Every stroke count I took for this chapter was taken from Olympic swimming races (50 meter pool), thus for you to make comparisons you must be in a 50 meter pool.

Note: when counting, be sure to include the first half-stroke which takes place under the water before your breakout.

Which to train first? Technique or tempo?

Some of you may now have a fire in your belly to get to the pool immediately and start working on a 1.3-1.4 tempo rate. That might sound like a great idea, especially for the Type-A personalities in the group. STOP! SLOW DOWN. Do not go the route of the 8 & Under swimmer. Remember, that does not work any better than a long glide.

"Power and speed" are not the same as "hurrying and rushing." Olympic swimmers have developed the vital element of FEEL, and they always hold the water with a high elbow. Please trust me when I say that the turnover speed can be developed later. You must first develop an entirely new muscle memory if you have never thought about a high elbow and feel before. This requires thoughtful concentration. Within a few months, if you have controlled yourself, then you will be ready to start thinking about power, speed, and the RATE side of the equation.

Interestingly enough, for those of you who have been gliding or doing an exaggerated S-pull, your tempo will actually automatically speed up simply by taking a more efficient pull path through the water. It will feel strange and almost "wrong", because the rhythm to which you were so accustomed is now going to change. Work with the new rhythm. It is not wrong; it is right. Do not bail out of making a beneficial change just because it "doesn't feel right." I am calling you out on this again like I did in Chapter 6. Do not be product oriented. Focus on the process.

1996 and 2008 Olympic stroke rate and stroke count examples

The following pages present a compilation of stroke rates and stroke counts of specific Olympic medalists in various freestyle events. The numbers were gathered as I sat in my living room and replayed video from the 1996 Olympics in Atlanta and the 2008 Olympics in Beijing. I make no claim that the numbers are accurate to the hundreth of a second, but they are close enough so as to make relevant conclusions on certain matters.

Also, some of the information I present is more complete on certain swimmers than others. This is simply due to the TV coverage. Often I was unable to count strokes on a field of swimmers when the TV camera panned in on the leader for any significant period of time. In those cases, I present as much information as was possible to gather.

Lastly, since these numbers are taken from actual Olympic swimming races, the pool length was 50 meters. If you are interested in comparing your stroke count to that of an Olympic swimmer, for example, then you need to be in a 50 meter pool. The counts are not the same if you swim in a 25 meter pool and double the number, due to the turn at the wall.

I hope you enjoy seeing how the equation, # Strokes x Rate, plays out among various Olympic swimmers.

Let's look at the women first

The following numbers do not include the first 50 meters due to the distance generated by the starting dive.

1996 Olympic gold medalist, 800 Free, Brooke Bennett of the USA (8:27.89): Brooke on average took 26 to 26.5 stroke cycles per 50 meters at a rate of approximately 1.15

1996 Olympic silver medalist, 800 Free, Dagmar Hase of Germany (8:29.91): Dagmar on average took 24 stroke cycles per 50 meters at a rate of approximately 1.25

2008 Olympic gold medalist, 800 Free, Rebecca Adlington of Great Britain (8:14.10): Rebecca on average took 20 stroke cycles per 50 meters at a rate of 1.38-1.4

2008 Olympics: the 800 Meter Freestyle silver medalist, Filippi of Italy, stroked at a rate of 1.5-1.6, and the bronze medalist, Friis of Denmark, turned over at 1.35-1.4 seconds per cycle (stroke counts not available due to T.V. coverage)

1996 Olympic gold medalist, 200 Free, Claudia Poll of Costa Rica (1:58.16): Claudia on average took 25 stroke cycles per 50 meters at a rate of approximately 1.13

1996 Olympic silver medalist, 200 Free, Franciska Vanalmsnik of Germany (1:58.57): Franciska on average took 20 stroke cycles per 50 meters at a rate of approximately 1.4

2008 Olympic gold medalist, 200 Free, Federica Pellegrini of Italy (1:54.82): Federica on average took 21 to 21.5 stroke cycles per 50 meters at a rate of approximately 1.25 (note that in the 400 Meter Freestyle in Beijing, Pellegrini took 20.5 stroke cycles per 50 at a rate of 1.35)

2008 Olympics, fourth place, 200 Free, Katie Hoff of the USA (1:55.78): Katie on average took 20-20.5 stroke cycles per 50 meters at a rate of approximately 1.3

The 2008 USA women's 4 x 200 free relay bronze medalists all stroked in the range of 1.3. The Australian gold medalists in the same relay stroked in the range of 1.2-1.4

2008 Olympics: Dara Torres of the USA, on the 2nd 50 meters of the 100 free (on her leg of the 4 x 100 Meter Freestyle Relay), took 20 strokes at a rate of 1.25

Now let's look at the men's events

2008 Olympic gold medalist, 400 Free, Tae Hwan Park of Korea (3:41.86): Park on average took 17 stroke cycles per 50 meters at a rate of approximately 1.5 (on the last 100 meters, Park stroked at a rate of 1.3)

2008 Olympic bronze medalist, 400 Free, Larsen Jensen of the USA (3:42.78): Larsen on average took 17 stroke cycles per 50 meters at a rate of approximately 1.55 (on the last 100 meters, Larsen stroked at a rate of 1.3. His stroke count went to 19.5)

1996 Olympic gold medalist, 200 Free, Daniel Loader of New Zealand (1:47.63): Daniel on average took 19.5 stroke cycles per 50 meters at a rate of approximately 1.3

2008 Olympic gold medalist, 200 Free, Michael Phelps of the USA (1:42.96): Michael on average took 14.5 stroke cycles per 50 meters at a rate of 1.5-1.55

2008 Olympic silver medalist, 200 Free, Park Tae Hwan of Korea (1:44.85): Park on average took 18 stroke cycles per 50 meters at a rate of approximately 1.35

1996 Olympic gold medal 4 x 200 Meter Freestyle Relay team, of the USA: The average number of strokes cycles per 50 meters among all four swimmers was 18 to 19, and their strokes rates were consistently in the range of 1.35-1.4

2008 Olympic gold medalist, during his anchor leg of the 4 x 200 Meter Freestyle Relay, Peter Vanderkaay of the USA (relay split 1:44.7): Peter on average took 16.5 stroke cycles per 50 meters at a rate of approximately 1.55

It is interesting to note that Peter changed his stroke rate throughout the 200. Below is a recap of each 50 meters:
1st 50: 14 strokes at 1.55 (consider the dive off the blocks when looking at stroke count)
2nd 50: 15 strokes at 1.55
3rd 50: 16.5 strokes at 1.4
4th 50: 17.5 strokes at 1.35-1.38

2008 Olympic gold medalist, 100 Free, Alain Bernard of France (47.21): Alain took 20 stroke cycles on his 2nd 50 meters, at a rate of approximately 1.1 (Bernard stayed under water after the turn for approximately 2.5 seconds)

2008 Olympic bronze medalist, 100 Free, Jason Lezak of the USA(47.67): Jason took 18 stroke cycles on his 2nd 50 meters at a rate of 1.25-1.3 (Jason stayed under water after the turn for approximately 3.1 seconds)

General notes

1. Please note that the number of stroke cycles per 50 meters is, in part, affected by how long a swimmer stays underwater kicking off the turns. International rules allow for a maximum of 15 meters. Most swimmers in the 200 freestyle and longer events do not stay under for the full 15 meters (due to oxygen requirements), but some stay under particularly longer than others. Michael Phelps, for instance, kicked under water for more than 4 seconds, while silver medalist Tae Hwan Park of Korea was under water for approximately 2.5 seconds after the turns. The length of time under water obviously affects the stroke count.

2. Also note, when taking stroke rates, the variations in time from stroke to stroke, even within one 50 meter length, can vary slightly due to a number of factors (i.e., was the swimmer taking a breath; was fatigue setting in; and natural factors such as the fact that we are measuring humans, not machines).

3. In the mid to long distance freestyle events (200 to 800) the stroke rates for women have stayed in the general range from 1.1 cycles per second to 1.45 cycles per second.

4. Men's stroke rates are generally longer than women's. Middle-distance and distance men (200 to 1500) have stroke rates that fall primarily in the range 1.30-1.60

5. Ian Thorpe (the Thorpedo) of Australia on average took 15.5 stroke cycles at a rate of approximately 1.6.

6. At the 1996 Olympics, I stroked at a rate of 1.25 in the 200 Meter Freestyle in the pool; whereas, at the 2000 Olympics in triathlon (open water swimming) my rate was in the range of 1.3-1.5 depending on the waves and water conditions.

Peter Vanderkaay, reminding us of the high-elbow position that must be held under the water in order to optimize the stroke count and rate equation.

Summary for Chapter 7

1. (# Strokes) x (Rate) = TIME

2. The fastest swimmers in the world turnover at a rate of 1.0-1.6 seconds per full stroke cycle.

3. Swimmers who attempt to reduce their stroke count by gliding out front have rates of turnover between 2.0-3.0 seconds per full stroke cycle.

4. The top swimmers are able to reduce their stroke count without increasing their rate of turnover, because they "hold" the water in a high-elbow position and pull their bodies over their hands. Their rate of turnover is fast, because their hand did not take a long path out front nor a long, meandering S-pull path under the water.

We are finished with Chapter 7, but I would like to give you a test. Below are photographs of four underwater holds. Three are correct; one is incorrect. Can you tell which is the incorrect underwater arm position?

I can't help but sing the Sesame Street tune when I look at this square. I loved that game! Whenever it came on I totally bowled over my twin brother to get to the TV screen first.

"One of these things is not like the others,
One of these things just doesn't belong.
Can you tell which thing is not like the others,
By the time I finish my song?"

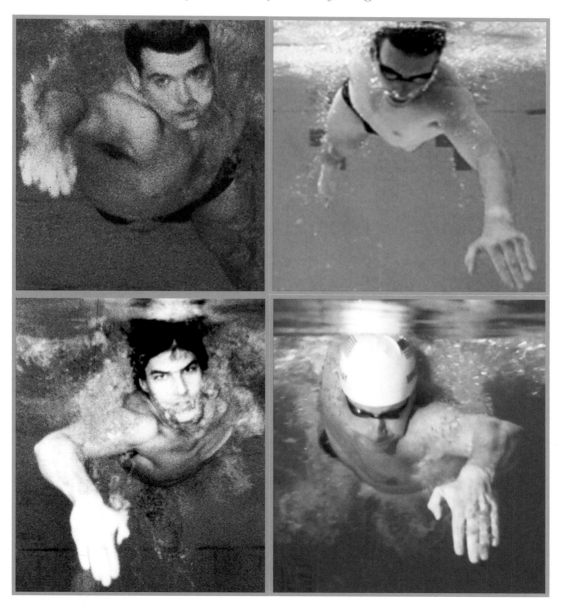

The two pictures above depict a side view of the "low elbow." Note that Jim has an ideal body position, head position, hip rotation and timing. The only thing missing is the high-elbow, which is the key to propulsion and rate of turnover.

The subject of the "low elbow" is Jim, a dear friend of mine. He is 37 years old, strong, fit, a fantastic marathon runner (2:56:58), and triathlete, and as you can see he has great body position, head position, hip roll, and timing; yet he averages 1:29 per 100 yards when doing a 30 minute swim at best effort. That is good for someone who did not grow up swimming, but his potential is to be 15 seconds faster per 100 if he would take the same amount of time he now spends in the water (3 days per week on good weeks) and focus solely on the high-elbow position and feel.

The number of strokes Jim takes to get across the pool is the same as what I take, but his rate of turnover is 1.9 seconds per full stroke cycle, swimming at his triathlon race pace. He attempts to get a fairly long reach/extension during the front phase of his stroke and then pushes downward with his hand to get to a depth to pull back under his body. His arm/elbow stays straight during the early phase of the stroke (no high elbow). My rate of turnover at the same effort is 1.3. I am not trying any harder to get that faster turnover; instead I am getting into the high-elbow position early in the stroke so as to hold the water in a way that will move me forward. I have no glide out front, nor is my hand taking a long path under the water. My hand takes a predominantly direct path below me, with slight impulses/sculls that find the still water.

If the 6/10s second per stroke cycle difference is multiplied by the number of strokes taken for a 100 freestyle (approximately 8 full strokes per 25 yards), then I will be 4.8 seconds faster per 25 yards (8 strokes x .6 rate = 4.8). That will translate into 19.2 seconds per 100 yards. I will also gain time on him during the streamlines off the wall (another .5 to one second per turn most likely), because he does not work each streamline 100% in practice, having never fully considered the benefits and importance of it.

By the way, are you wondering how you email a friend and ask if they are willing to be the subject of how *not* to do something? There were about 100 people I could have called who have the same low elbow. The only one I knew who would not take it personally was Jim, because he has a great sense of humor and humble spirit. Plus, I promised him that I would inform readers that he could beat me in any distance running race and any bike sprint for a city limit sign.

Chapter 8
Piecing it All Together
conclusions and "calling the suit"

We are at the end of the book, and I am worried about one thing. I am worried that I made my point so well about the pull being the vital factor that you are all like Frankenstein monsters now. While I can't picture quite how it will go over, I am nervous that you are going to show up to practice and cause havoc at your swim team or triathlon group, insisting that Pareto be honored. It's either going to be that, or I am going to be at a triathlon or swim meet one day and see you swimming like Tarzan. Don't do that please.

Actually, I take that back...if you win the 100 Freestyle at your next swim meet, or if you lead out of T-1 at your next triathlon, swimming like Johnny Weissmuller, then I am going to be the first to shake your hand.

Seriously though, remember to keep everything in context. Yes, the pull is the vital factor. Without it you are never going to be a really fast swimmer; however, there are a number of other components to stroke technique that you must address as well. The other 80% do impact our performance, so they deserve a percentage of our attention. None will get the leading role like the pull gets, but the others are either supporting actors/actresses or part of the behind-the-scenes crew.

Our supporting actors and actresses are things such as hip roll, the kick, and using the body core to accentuate power. These things do not make for a good story on their own, but at the same time, the real character of the pull is not fully revealed without them.

The behind-the-scenes crew includes elements of the stroke such as knowing how to breathe and establishing a body position on top of the water. Without these the door to the theatre would never be unlocked. For this reason they cannot be minimized, especially for beginners, but I encourage a mindset that recognizes we need to move past these at the moment we have established a comfort with the water.

As a supplement to the main text, I wrote about a few of the non-vital elements in Appendix C ("Answers to Common Questions"). The extent to which I address these elements goes only so far as to show how they tie in with the underwater pull, because the basics are thoroughly explained on dozens of websites and in every swim technique book at the bookstore. There was no need for me to rewrite what is already available.

My mission was to fill the gaping hole that has existed since humans first took to competitive swimming. This book was born out of recognition that someone had to sort the overwhelming amount of information for you. More than that, the real intent was to introduce you to the thinking tools that guide you to sort information for yourself. The tools apply to any area of your life that involves productivity goals.

What does 80% and 20% of the time really mean?

Below is an example of how, during a workout, I applied a portion of my 20% focus on the 80% of non-vital technique aspects of freestyle. Since many people over-emphasize body position considerations in practice, I chose this particular element to demonstrate.

Below are four situations in training when my focus was on body position:

1. As a "check": Sporadically in the middle of a swim set, I would check my position. Especially if I was fatiguing toward the end of workout, I would turn my attention to whether or not my core was staying strong and my head steady. The "check" took a fraction of a second. Our body position is much less dynamic than our pulling arms, so once we establish the position we want, we need only hold it there with minimal concentration.

2. As a tool to ensure my stroke had power: I turned my attention to my core in order to drive power into my stroke, if the swim set was meant to be done with speed and power. This had more to do with getting a desired training effect than technique. In these instances I primarily worked the high-elbow aspect of the pull, but I was also cognizant of holding a strong tone in my core and a quicker tempo of my rotating hips. The hips must keep pace with arm turnover; therefore, if you speed up arm turnover during a sprint, then the hip roll must become more dynamic as well.

3. As a stroke technique drill: I almost always chose drills that involved a high elbow and feel for the water, but every once in a while I would work on a different aspect of the stroke, such as hip roll. However, whereas many people think about hip roll as a method of reducing resistance, I encourage swimmers to think of it primarily in terms of rhythmically accentuating the pull.

4. On the tow machine: The tow machine is a unique tool that is not readily available to most people. I feel fortunate to have had access to it occasionally. A swimmer wears a belt around his/her waist, and a cable is attached from the belt to a pulley system above the water. The pulley system can be set to any speed the swimmer/coach chooses, even as fast as the men's 50 meter freestyle world record. The swimmer may either hold a streamline position as he/she is pulled the length of the pool, or the swimmer may try to stroke at a rate fast enough to keep up with the machine. There is no tool in swimming that shines a light more brightly on the Theoretical Square Law (resistance increasing exponentially as velocity increases). I have been on a tow machine approximately 12 times in my swimming career, for a lifetime total of only 4 hours perhaps.

Contrast the occasional focus of body position to the amount of concentration placed on the pull. From the moment I dove in the water for warm-up I thought about a high-elbow position and feel for the water. It remained at the forefront of concentration throughout the entire workout. Even if the position becomes natural for a swimmer there is still a need to work the range of motion of the position along with the strength that goes into holding the water. FEEL for the water is not only the most important part of the stroke, but it is also the most enjoyable. As swimmers, we are fortunate that our sport affords us the gift of enjoying what is most important for success.

How to take it from here

Even though you probably already have a good idea about how to proceed in your plan now, the following 3 sections of this chapter include my advice for the 3 types of readers I assume have picked up this book:

1. Adults learning to swim
2. Experienced swimmers who have had success but want to know what it takes to reach the next level.
3. Swimmers and triathletes who have worked on body position and gliding as their vital element for years.

Specific advice for adults learning to swim: As mentioned, some aspects of the free-style swim stroke are out-right necessary for beginners to learn before anything else, such as comfort in the water and breathing. Those will be your vital elements for a short while. There is absolutely no reason though why a beginner cannot do dry land exercises (tubing, Halo, and press-outs) and a few in-water drills (sculling, even if simply standing like Gary Hall Jr. did) to develop feel and a high elbow.

Coaches who work with adults learning to swim should have compassion for the challenges of establishing a comfort level in the water, but should also not underestimate their swimmer's ability to handle the most advanced elements of the swim stroke. Even if a woman approached me and said that she was 70 years old, had never done an athletic event in her life, but wanted to learn to swim in order to compete in a triathlon, I would introduce her to tubing and sculling on the first day.

Every person, no matter their age, level of experience, or level of strength and flexibility, is capable of making progress toward the vital elements of swimming.

P.S. For those of you who are not yet comfortable with the water, please review the section on sculling regularly. Take note of the way the hands are held - with tone, not cupped. Place your focus on FEELING the pressure of the water on your forearms and hands, and you will begin to have a calm control over your body in the water. Panic comes when we fight the water and become rigid, so slow down and focus on the feel. If you do this, then you will see the sport from an entirely new perspective, and your comfort level will improve dramatically.

Specific advice for experienced swimmers who have had success but want to know what it takes to reach the next level: If you are an experienced swimmer, even at the collegiate/ NCAA level, you should be concentrating the majority of your technique focus on feel, hold, and the high-elbow during aerobic sets, endurance sets, anaerobic sets, sprinting, warm-up/warm-down, and every other set. The position can always be developed for more range and strength, even if you think you are doing it quite well already. I wish I knew, back in my high school and college days, how to do that. All the lengths up and down the pool, when I was alone with my thoughts, could have actually been applied to something useful instead of thinking about being hungry, or that the water was cold, or how I could not wait until the 2 hour practice was over.

Swim with focus. Make each practice count. Know why you do what you do, everyday. If you have a rough day, do not be hard on yourself; make something of it. Even if you are fatigued to the point of not making the intervals, then think about streamlining, holding the water, or gaining range of motion in the high-elbow position. You should leave every practice able to specifically verbalize, "I just became better today, because..."

Your greatest gains will come when you work the high-elbow and hold during anaerobic or lactate sets (all-out swims). Many athletes spend energy trying to think of ways to avoid the pain during these sets when they should be focusing on strengthening the underwater pull (and the kick for those who are 6 beat kickers... see Appendix C for information on the kick).

Also, meet with your coach to discuss stroke tempo. Analyze your rate compared to the rates of Olympic medalists (Chapter 7). You are in charge of figuring out how to optimize the two factors of the swimming equation. It is all logic and common sense, around which a specific plan may be built. Start building that plan today.

Lastly, be honest; be ethical. I could never fully understand the psyche of a person who feels a great sense of accomplishment knowing they enhanced their performance illegally. It is naive to believe that winning is a ticket to happiness. Convictions and moral code trump a gold medal every time. Develop those before your swim stroke.

Be strong
Race clean

Specific advice for swimmers and triathletes who have worked body position and gliding as their vital element for years: Simply stated, within this group, a revolution needs to take place. If you fall into this category, then your mindset must be flipped on its head. In order to move quickly through the water, you are going to have to design a plan that works the underwater pull the majority of the time...80% of the time. Throw your obsession with gliding, streamlining, and reducing resistance right out the window. It is making you slow. Trade it in for increasing resistance on the water underneath you, for the sake of traction.

The information on stroke rates and stroke counts of Olympic swimmers from the previous chapter has always been available. I am baffled at how it has not been the center of every swimming technique discussion. If it had been, then I believe the past 15 years would have proved more productive for the swimmers who have been wondering what they are missing.

The only thing you were missing was the full story. Believe it or not, that is good news. You now have the information that should infuse a new round of enthusiasm into your workouts again. Be sure to focus on technique before building the rate side of the equation. You have plenty of time. Do not rush the process. Those of you who understand that a strong underwater pull takes time are going to succeed at swimming fast; whereas those who rush the process will remain frustrated.

One more group: There will be some of you who, after reading everything that is involved with going fast, choose a long, gliding, less taxing swim stroke for your style. You may not be concerned with speed and winning. You may just want to enjoy the sport for all of its other benefits. Beautiful. I admire you for calling the suit, and I would be your euchre partner anytime.

Applying thought processes to training - knowing what to work on and when

We know that strength and conditioning provide little benefit unless a swimmer is holding the water, so the underwater pull must be developed before anything else. Once the technique is established training becomes more of a critical factor. Methodologies in training are as numerous as technique elements of the swim stroke, so again we are faced with sorting through massive amounts of information in order to identify which elements are vital.

A young athlete may need to build an aerobic base; whereas, an experienced, older swimmer with a well-established aerobic base may identify that speed is the critical factor. Swimmers and coaches should look at the big picture and determine which aspects of training are most crucial.

Multi-sport athletes have to manage the big picture even more than single sport athletes. Knowing when to back off training one discipline in order to have energy for training another discipline is challenging. Applying the reasoning that underlies the 80/20 Rule is useful in sorting through the choices, as is The Law of Diminishing Returns.

Also, be sure to re-evaluate your situation on a regular basis. You are never the same athlete from season to season. Hopefully you are different for having developed new strengths over the course of a year. Know yourself and the cards you are dealt, and then make confident decisions from there.

Answering the question from the introduction

To wrap things up, do you see why the elite swimming world is breaking records left and right? They are optimizing the equation from Chapter 2. They are taking fewer strokes at a faster rate, and accomplishing it via an amazing hold on the water below. Their focus is in the deep blue, third dimension.

You will be hard-pressed to find an elite swimmer who is not a hard worker, but you must recognize that his/her strength training and conditioning are only meaningful because of the hold. The masses of swimmers and triathletes who train diligently day after day and see no improvement in their times are facing their dilemma due to the fact that they have nothing solid upon which to place the hard work. We can correct this, thank goodness.

You may not have a six-figure sponsorship, nor access to the top training equipment that some elite athletes have, but you have access to the same water. Water does not discriminate. It is there for the taking. So, do what Johnny Weissmuller did, and get a purchase on the elusive.

This is your life! You may get euchred if you take a risk, but at least you boldly played the game.

What does it mean, "getting euchred?" It means that you called the trump suit, but your competition was dealt a better hand and beat you. It happens occasionally (I got euchred during the fencing portion of the pentathlon in Beijing). Haha. It was still worth it!

CALL THE SUIT!!!

Book Summary

1. Faster swimming requires optimizing the equation: # Strokes x Rate = TIME

2. The underwater pull is the vital factor that determines the # Strokes and the Rate.

3. 80% of a swimmer's focus should be on the underwater pull.

4. Every person, no matter what age or what level swimmer, is capable of gaining the strength, flexibility and feel for the water required for forward propulsion.

5. Strength and conditioning will mean something once you have a hold on the water.

80 / 20 . . . the vital few . . . THE UNDERWATER PULL . . .

high elbow . . . FEEL . . . propulsion . . . #STROKES x RATE = TIME . . .

tubing . . . HALO . . . press outs . . . SCULLING . . . . streamlines .

LAW OF DIMINISHING RETURNS . . . theoretical square law . . . TONE . . .

still water . . . BE BRAVE . . . call the suit . . . PURCHASE THE ELUSIVE . . .

THE UNDERWATER PULL . . . high elbow . . . FEEL . . . . sculling

Appendix A
One Last Toast
1924 to 2008

Below is a Top 20 list of everything I could think of, or was led to discover during the research for this book, that appears to be a contributing factor in the improvement of swimming times since Weissmuller's day. It includes discoveries in technique, training methods, and inventions. I made this list for two reasons:

A) For fun. There is some great historical perspective in the list.

B) To toast Pareto one last time, because the 80/20 notation he made over 100 years ago stands true with regards to swimming technique and performance impact. If you take Weissmuller's 57.4 world record and compare it with the current world record set by Cesar Cielo of 46.9, there is a 20% differential. That proves that a powerful pull, which is the only common denominator between Weissmuller and Cielo, other than the fact that they both competed in water, is 80% of competitive swimming. Everything else on this list adds up to the other 20%.

Top 20 list of changes and developments in swimming between 1924 and 2008

1. **Starting blocks:** First used in 1936. Before that, swimmers dove off the side of the pool.

2. **Flip turns:** First came onto the scene in the 1950s.

3. **Shaving down:** First thought of as a way to reduce resistance in the 1950s by the Australians.

4. **Wind up starts:** Prior to the early 1970s swimmers did not grab the starting blocks.

5. **Entry angle of dive:** Weissmuller describes his entry into the water, and he truly believed it was superior. Below is his description:

"My starting plunge is worthy of a little extended study...my head is down and I am looking with open eyes at the water....One leg is raised much higher than the other. These things do not just happen; every point here means something. When I hit the water, I bring my arms down with a powerful slap, and at the same time I bring my raised leg down with a tremendous plop. I look at the water so as to time this slap of the arms and leg exactly at the moment of my entry into the water....Making the shallow plunge, keeping high in the water by slapping down with my arms and leg, I am ready to begin swimming sooner than my rivals." [1]

Also, remember the pike dive that was hugely popular into the '70s? It did nothing more for swimmers than Weissmuller's starting plunge, since both stop the explosive power from the push off the blocks almost immediately upon entry.

6. **Invention of competitive swimming goggles:** First introduced in the early 1970s,

goggles enhanced a swimmer's vision in the water. At the 1972 Olympics in Munich goggles were not allowed. The first Olympics with goggles–1976.

7. **Longer training sessions:** In addition to enhancing a swimmer's vision, goggles also impacted training methods. Swimmers could stay in the water longer, thus longer training sessions were possible, positively affecting aerobic capacities and endurance capabilities in swimmers.

8. **Advancements in Scientific Research:** In recent decades, sports science, psychology, training research, physiology labs, zone training, heart-rate training, bio-mechanical analysis, and the study of fluid dynamics have been funded for research to improve training methods and overall performance.

9. **Nutrition/hydration:** The availability of high-quality organic and natural foods, protein drinks, recovery foods, energy bars, and education on the importance of hydration, did not come on the scene until the 1980s. My twin brother reminded me that we never used water bottles when we swam in high school in the mid '80s.

10. **Body position/streamlining:** Weissmuller definitely thought he was onto something with his hydroplaning reasoning, but we have come a long way in truly understanding body position considerations. We have also learned a great deal about using the body core to accentuate the power that is generated from holding the water with the limbs.

11. **Strength training, core power training**: The focus on strength and core power today is significant compared to the 1980s and even the 1990s. You will be hard pressed to find any top collegiate swim program that does not have access to a state-of-the-art strength facility and specialized strength coaches.

12. **Inventions:** Power Racks, Power Tower, the Halo Bench, towing machines, monofins, in-water parachutes, and a number of other strength/power tools provide training options that were never available to swimmers prior to the 1980s.

13. **Team support at international events:** Team support has evolved into a full staff of massage therapists, physical therapists, sports psychologists, trainers, doctors, chiropractors, and physiologists - much more than Weissmuller would have had accompany him.

14. **Pool technology:** Lane lines, pool depth, and gutters are now thoughtfully designed to reduce surface resistance from waves.

15. **Swim suit technology:** Suits have evolved from baggy cotton trunks and wool, to nylon, to lycra, to materials that simulate shark skin. In addition, full body suits were introduced in the 1990s when it was discovered that an athlete's skin and muscle rippled when fluid forces acted upon it, thus a full body, tight-fitting suit would keep surface resistance of human tissue to a minimum.

16. **Marketing and Sponsorships allow athletes to compete for more years:** The paradigms on age and performance have taken a dramatic turn, in large part due to sports agents, marketing, and sponsorship dollars affording swimmers the opportunity to remain in sport much longer than was the case in Weissmuller's day.

17. **Larger talent pool:** As a result of the internet, the talent pool around the world now has access to the most current swimming theories, techniques, and training methods.

18. **Pool chemicals:** Salt water provides more buoyancy than tap water, so a pool with salt tablets would positively impact swimming times. I have done no study to determine which chemicals are used at international swimming competitions, or even if there are guidelines to regulate this; however, my first taste of water that seemed salty was in Sydney, Australia during the 2000 Olympics while training in a pool before the triathlon event. I wondered if salt tablets had been added to the water. It would be a logical and simple thing to do to improve swimming performance. Anyone know the answer?

19. **Performance enhancing drugs:** This is an unfortunate truth.

20. **Psychology to meet new standards:** As new world records are set, the bar is raised, and athletes will always look to raise the bar again. There is a psychology component to believing that new standards are possible once a mark is set.

So...

If Johnny Weissmuller had been able to take advantage of the 20 items listed above (except the performance enhancing drugs), then with the high-elbow pull he used, I am willing to bet he would be challenging for today's world record.

Those of us competing today have already benefitted from, or have access to, most of what is on the list (once again...not the performance enhancing drugs). We train long hours in the pool to develop aerobic capacities and endurance capabilities, do strength work, eat healthy foods, hydrate, buy the most expensive swim suits, streamline, shave down, perfect our starts and turns, and so on, but...not one of those efforts will put us in a position to challenge the elite ranks who are tearing up the pool if we do not first have the PULL.

I wish you a wonderful new experience in swimming as you embark on discovering the third dimension that lies below you in the water. Enjoy your new-found propulsive power.

Appendix B

For Beginners

understanding swimming lingo and workout design

For those of you who are new to swimming, this appendix is a quick review of some common terms as well as an explanation of how swim team workouts are designed. After reading this appendix, you will be able to jump in with any team and understand the flow of practice.

Short Course vs. Long Course

There are 3 different sized pools in the competitive swimming circles:

1. Short course yards: this is 25 YARD pool
2. Short course meters: this is a 25 METER pool
3. Long course meters: this is a 50 METER pool

In essence, any swimming pool that is recognized for competitive purposes is either measured in yards or meters, and, to go one step further, if thinking in international terms, then meters is really the only pertinent measurement. The United States is the one country that hosts competitions in a "yard" pool.

Also, there is no such thing as a 50 YARD pool. If there is one somewhere, then it is not one which is recognized in the competitive swimming community.

The key to pool length terminology is that "short course" refers to a shorter pool, one that is 25 in length, whether measured in yards or meters. "Long course" implies a longer pool, hence the distance of "50" associated with it.

If you look at swim meet results, the front page will always (at least it should) indicate if the meet was contested in one of the three lengths. The abbreviations are as follows:

1. For short course yards (a pool the length of 25 yards): "SCY"

2. For short course meters (a pool the length of 25 meters): "SCM"

3. For long course meters (a pool the length of 50 meters): "LCM"

Distinguishing a 25 yard pool from a 25 meter pool may seem obvious, since a meter is approximately 10% longer than a yard. A 100 Meter Freestyle will be approximately 10% more distance to cover than a 100 Yard Freestyle. While the need for distinction between yards and meters is fairly obvious, the part that confuses some people is why swimmers would need to distinguish between a 100 Meter Freestyle held in a 50 meter pool (LCM) versus a 100 Meter Freestyle held in a 25 meter pool (SCM), since the distance covered is the same.

The reason the distinction must be made is due to the flip turns. In a 25 meter pool there are 3 turns for the 100 Meter Freestyle; whereas, in a 50 meter pool there is only 1 turn. Since a swimmer generates a great amount of power off the solid wall, the times in a 25 meter pool are faster than in a 50 meter pool.

A Few Notes on Swimming Pool Lengths

1. The Olympics is always contested as LCM - in a 50 meter pool.

2. Most high school and collegiate competitions in the United states are contested SCY - in a 25 yard pool.

3. The international organizing body for swimming, FINA, began to recognize SCM world records - those set in a 25 meter pool - in the early 1990s. Before then, only LCM world records were recognized.

Workouts - how they are designed

Workouts in swimming generally follow the same format, no matter which team you join. The workout as a whole is divided into a number of "sets." A set is simply a number of repeats either on a send-off interval or on a rest-interval. What is a send-off interval and a rest-interval?

Send-off interval: This is the most common way to design a set in swimming. Let's use an example: if a coach tells the team that the next set is going to be 10 x 100 on the 2:00, that means the swimmers leave at the 2 minute mark to start the next 100. Some swimmers may finish their 100 in 1:15, so they will get 45 seconds rest before leaving on the 2:00 send-off. Other swimmers may finish their 100 in 1:40; therefore, they will get 20 seconds rest before the next 100. This obviously does not seem fair that the faster swimmers get more rest, so that is why swim teams divide swim-

mers into lanes based on speed. The faster swimmers will have tougher send-off times. Swimming is a great sport in this sense; there is always a lane for you no matter what your speed. As you get faster, you move up to faster lanes.

Rest-interval: Another way to design a set is to give the swimmers a certain amount of rest after each repeat. The coach may say, "We are going to do 10 x 100 with 30 seconds rest after each one." This means that, even within one lane, swimmers may be leaving at different times. Track workouts are often designed with rest intervals.

Swim workout lingo

1) A coach may say, "We are going to do 10 x 100 on 2:00, descending 1-5 and 6-10." The "descending 1-5 and 6-10" means that team members are to swim slightly faster on each 100 from number 1 to number 5 and then slow down again on number 6 so that the time is similar to the first 100 of the first 5, but then get faster each of the 100s from 6 to 10.

Times in a descending set may look as follows:

#1: 1:30 (the swimmer will get 30 seconds rest before leaving on the 2:00)
#2: 1:27 (the swimmer will get 33 seconds rest before leaving on the 2:00)
#3: 1:25
#4: 1:21
#5: 1:18 (this is the fastest of the first 5…the swimmer gets 42 seconds rest before leaving on the 2:00)
#6: 1:30 (this is intended to be easy, like #1)
#7: 1:28
#8: 1:24
#9: 1:22
#10: 1:17 (this is the fastest of the second 5)

2) Another common term in swimming is "building." To use the same example as the set above, if a coach says, "We are going to do 10 x 100 on the 2:00 building each one," then that means to get faster as the 100 progresses. In other words, the first 25 would be easy, and then the second 25 faster, the third 25 even faster, and the final 25 the fastest. You build your speed as the 100 progresses.

This is different than descending, because in descending there is no change-up of speed within the 100; the change of speed only takes place from one 100 to the next. In building, all 10 of the 100 meter or yard repeats will be similar in overall time (for instance, the swimmer may swim around a 1:26 on each 100), but the coach should see a marked difference in the speed between the first 25 and the last 25 of each.

3) The final term used in swimming that will help you to know is "negative splitting." This means that the second half of a repeat should be faster than the first half. Going to our example, if a coach says, "We are going to do 10 x 100 on the 2:00 negative split," then this is similar to building in the sense that the times on each 100 of the set will usually be around the same (as opposed to descending), but negative splitting is different that building in that there is a crisp, clear change of speed at the half-way point of the repeat.

In a negative split swim, the swimmer will have one speed for the first 50 and then change immediately to the faster speed for the second 50. Building is a gradual change of speed throughout the 100; whereas, negative splitting is an abrupt change at the half-way point.

An example of a workout

Warm-up 800 choice (this means you can do any stroke you want, or kick, pull, whatever for an 800, no interval)

4 x 150 @ 2:50 (first 50 drill / second 50 kick with no board / third 50 build freestyle)... you would be able to understand this, because you know what "build" means for that last 50 of each repeat. You would also know that the 2:50 is your send-off interval.

20 x 25 @ :50 ALL OUT your choice of stroke

8 x 100 free, swim, descend 1-4 and 5-8 @ 2:00

10 x 50 Kick your choice of stroke, negative split (make the second 25 FAST), :20 rest after each 50

Warm-down 200 easy

Total distance: 3400
Total time: appx. 1 1/4 hour to 1 1/2 hours

That's it. All of the sets between the warm-up and warm-down are intended to train various energy systems, strokes, and techniques. If you know about send-offs, rest intervals, descending, building, and negative splitting, then you can hang with any team in the world. Nuances of individual coaching styles can be picked up easily.

Be aware of which length pool you visit if you are on vacation or business, because you may wonder why you are going slower when you normally train in a 25 yard pool but then find yourself in a 25 meter pool unknowingly.

Appendix C
Answers to Common Questions

1. Breathing: Is it better to alternate-breathe, or breathe to just one side?

Many coaches will tell you that it is important to alternate breathe in order to develop a balanced, even stroke. The truth of the matter is that it does not matter. There are many top swimmers who alternate-breathe and also many who breathe every stroke on one side. You are a unique individual who has an internal rhythm, as well as comfort level for how much oxygen you need. If you breathe to one side only and your distance per stroke is not affected, nor your rate of turnover, then you have no worries.

I prefer alternate breathing. It happens to be the perfect rhythm for me, and gives the right amount of oxygen. But breathing patterns are not the vital element to the swim stroke.

If you do choose to incorporate alternate breathing into your stroke then be aware that it will feel awkward for the first few weeks. After those few weeks however, it will end up feeling quite natural and rhythmic. Also, be aware that your normal breathing side will always feel better than the other side.

2. Kicking: How important is it? Should I do a 6-beat kick or a 2-beat kick?

The answer to this question is similar to the answer above - you are a unique individual so your kick should match the rhythm of your stroke. Some of the top swimmers have a 2-beat kick and others have a 6-beat kick.

The swimmers who have a 2-beat kick tend to have shorter strokes. They get less distance per stroke but have much quicker turnovers. The 2-beat kick provides little or no propulsion. In fact, the swimmer primarily need only ensure that the kick does not get in the way of the speed generated by the arm stroke.

A swimmer with a 6-beat kick will tend toward a longer extension reach of their stroke out front (NOT a glide). The 6-beat kick aids the arm and shoulder strength requirements necessary to get into the high-elbow position from such an extended position. The kick, in other words, provides a supportive-like propulsion during this strenuous portion of the catch.

While a 6-beat kick is not a prerequisite to swimming fast, I believe there is a trend in the elite swimming world toward a 6-beat kick, and I believe that it is due to the relatively recent emphasis of strength training in the top programs. The advances made in strength training lend to a shoulder strength that is nicely supported by, and that nicely supports, a 6-beat kick. The benefits of this are that swimmer with a 6-beat kick has more options for stroke rate adjustments during a race. That swimmer may base his or her race strategy around a longer tempo during the first half of a race and a quicker tempo during the last half (or the last 50).

Take the Men's 200 Meter Freestyle in Beijing for example: Peter Vanderkaay, bronze medalist, swam the first 100 meters of the 200 at a tempo near 1.6 seconds per full stroke cycle. On the 3rd 50 he quickened his tempo approximately 1/10 second faster per cycle, and on the last 50 meters he quickened his tempo another 1/10 second to approximately 1.4 seconds per cycle. This was not a haphazard situation; it was a well thought-out race strategy.

Triathletes in a longer open water swim should not be concerned with changing tempo during a race. Settling into a consistent stroke rate for the entire swim is ideal unless there is a strategy to separate from the pack at some point.

How to kick: If you have a 2-beat kick, then it is not important to know how to kick. The goal is to keep the legs balanced, in rhythm with the arm cycle, and out of the way. The technique of kicking is much more important for 6-beat kickers.

Ankle flexibility is a big indicator of whether or not you will have a strong kick. Just as our forearm and hand "hold" the water, so our foot and lower leg should too. The theories of propulsion that we discussed earlier apply just as much to kicking as they do to pulling. Feel the resistive forces against your foot and lower leg. Hold the water as you apply a propulsive force to it. Ankle flexibility is required in order to hold the water in this manner.

The only way to get a hold of the water in freestyle kicking is to have the knee slightly bent on the down-kick. Look at the photo on this page. The leg applying force to the water is bent. If the knee is not bent, then the leg is like a wooden board pushing up and down against the water. This gives zero forward propulsion. Next time you go to a pool and kick, think about the "hold" on the water, with a supple, pliable foot and leg, applying force in a direction that moves you forward. The strength will come from your hip flexor and upper leg, but it is the foot and lower leg that hold the water.

A strong freestyle kick requires ankle flexibility, a bent leg down-kick, and a straight leg up-kick.

After finishing the down-kick it is extremely important to keep the leg straight on the up-kick, unless you are one of the rare people who are able to hyper-extend the knees. Assuming you are not one of those people - if you bend the leg on the up-kick, then you are applying pressure to the water in the opposite direction of what you just did on the down-kick.

Although next to impossible to believe, there are a fair number of triathletes and swimmers who actually move backward when they kick because of a bent knee up-kick. The answer for this frustrated crew is to simply focus on not bending the knee on the up-kick. A straight leg up-kick will, at minimum, keep them from going backward, and if they go one step further and concentrate on holding the water with their foot and leg on the down-kick, they might enjoy forward propulsive kicking for the very first time in their life. This is always cause for great celebration!

3. The use of fins in training - good or bad?

- For beginners: **BAD**
- For swimmers who want to feel fast without feeling the water and doing the work: **BAD**
- For swimmers who are looking for a power/strength training workout: **GOOD**

Using fins as a crutch is the worst thing a swimmer can do, and I see them used in this manner frequently. New swimmers who should be learning to feel the water will often times put on fins (or be told by a coach who does not understand the importance of true propulsive forces to put them on) as a way to give confidence. This slows the learning process, because every moment you are using fins means that you have lost that moment for developing true FEEL.

There are many wonderful drills and exercises that beginners can do to develop the true feel for the water, as were shared in Chapter 6. Please apply those and enjoy the journey that makes you an authentic swimmer.

The other group of people who are equally as guilty of using fins as a crutch are swimmers and triathletes who are 100% product oriented. They are primarily concerned with winning at practice, or at minimum keeping up with the people in their lane. They want to go fast at the races, but there is no long term view for crafting an amazingly propulsive stroke that will help them accomplish this.

There are only two groups of people who should be training with fins:

1. The people who swim for exercise and recreation: If the use of fins brings this group more enjoyment, then wonderful. They were never concerned with speed in the first place. They know their purpose, and they have called the suit.

2. Swimmers and triathletes who intend to purposefully build a specific training effect: Competitive swimmers and triathletes who understand the high-elbow and have developed a feel for the water with both their arms and legs know that the use of fins can be valuable for building strength, endurance, and power. They do not use the fins as a false sense of security. They use them for a specific training effect.

Note: There is one particular situation during which it is appropriate for new swimmers, or anyone for that matter, to use fins in order to "keep up" with other people during training. If you attend an open water swim session with a group of people who are faster than you, and if the fins allow you to keep up with the group, then you should definitely use them. No person should swim in the open water alone.

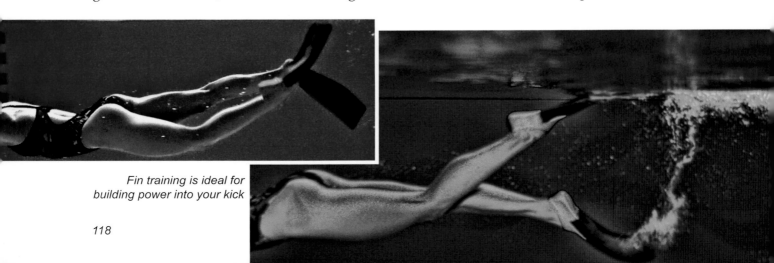

Fin training is ideal for building power into your kick

4. Hip roll - how much is too much or too little?

Just as the S-pull pattern has been taken to extremes by some swimmers (from Chapter 5), so too has the idea of rolling the hips. It is like the "telephone game" we all played as children - one person whispers in the ear of the person sitting next to them a short message, and the message then gets spread around the room in whispers until the last person states it out loud to the group. The numerous translations usually distort the message drastically.

Passing on swimming technique advice is no different than the telephone game. People everywhere, with very good intentions, repeat what they have heard from someone else about technique, but along the way vital information is left out or misinterpreted.

Hip roll is one of the components of technique that anyone can parrot to another person. In fact there is an entire scenario that plays out regularly each day around the world. It goes like this:

You are a new swimmer, and you go to the pool with a friend who has been swimming for a while. He/she is very kind to watch your stroke and give you a few pointers. You swim two lengths of the pool, and because you have never really swam before, and have never read a word about swim technique, you swim fairly flat - not much hip roll.

Your friend standing on the deck says to you, "You need to roll your hips." You have no idea how much to roll your hips. Your friend has no idea either, because he/she is just repeating what someone once told him/her. You figure, "more must be better," so you rotate so much that you almost tip over onto your back each time.

Now, if I was so bold as to interrupt this scenario, I would have attempted to stop the bleeding. I would not have had the energy to explain about propulsion, high elbows, and feel, but at least I would have stopped you from over rotating your hips. I would have explained the following:

If a swimmer over-rotates the hips, then every other part of the body must wait for the hips to finish. We need to remember that swimming is a synchronous sport; no component of the stroke can move at a rate faster than the others. The pull should determine your rate of turnover; therefore, every other aspect to your stroke should match the rhythm of that.

Hip-rolling in and of itself does not propel us forward. Try it. Get in the water with your arms either at your sides or our in front of you, and without applying force upon the water with your limbs, rotate your hips all you want. You will not move forward.

The most important function of the hip roll is to accentuate the power from the propulsive pull. Use the hips enough to maximize your power, but remember that additional hip roll beyond that not only gives zero return but is actually detrimental to the overall rate/turnover side of our important equation (# strokes x rate = TIME).

You do not even know what propulsion nor rate of turnover means, so you stare at me blankly. I just ruined your day, because you were feeling pretty good about yourself for having done so beautifully what your friend told you to do. I walk away thinking, "I need to write a book."

Notes

Introduction

1. Johnny Weissmuller (with Clarence A. Bush), *Swimming The American Crawl* (London: Putnam, 1930), p.45.

2. Ibid., p. 20.

Chapter 3: The Vital Element Revealed

1. Johnny Weissmuller (with Clarence A. Bush), *Swimming The American Crawl* (London: Putnam, 1930), p. 62.

2. Cecil M. Colwin, *Breakthrough Swimming* (Human Kinetics: United States, 2002), p. 109.

3. James E, Counsilman, *The Science of Swimming* (Prentice-Hall: Englewood Cliffs, 1968), pp. 16-17.

Chapter 4: Fluid Dynamics and Theories of Propulsion

1. Cecil M. Colwin, *Swimming Dynamics* (Masters Press: Chicago, 1999), p. 72.

2. Ibid., p. 78.

3. Cecil M. Colwin, *Swimming Into The 21st Century* (Leisure Press: Champaign, 1992), p. 20.

4. Cecil M. Colwin, *Swimming Dynamics* (Masters Press: Chicago, 1999), p. 74.

5. Ernest W. Maglischo, *Swimming Fastest* (Human Kinetics: United States, 2003), Preface and p. 18.

6. Ibid., p. 18.

Chapter 5: The Underwater Pull

1. Johnny Weissmuller (with Clarence A. Bush), *Swimming The American Crawl* (London: Putnam, 1930), p.15.

2. Ernest W. Maglischo, *Swimming Fastest* (Human Kinetics: United States, 2003), p. 18.

Appendix A : One Last Toast

1. Johnny Weissmuller (with Clarence A. Bush), *Swimming The American Crawl* (London: Putnam, 1930), p.27.

Resources

Halo Swim Training System (Halo bench and Sports Vector Tubing with SPHandle)
by Lane Gainer Sports - lanegainer.com   800-443-8946   craig@lanegainer.com

USA Triathlon - usatriathlon.org

USA Swimming - usaswimming.org

U.S. Masters Swimming - usms.org

International Swimming Hall of Fame - ishof.org

The Counsilman Center for The Science of Swimming - indiana.edu/~hplab/ccss.html

DREAMCATCHER: From heart to heart, from soul to soul, a swimmer can swim like a seed can grow....but where does it begin? from the brothers you race to the sisters who smile... and the mother that laughs as your father goes wild...that's the family you love...yet it starts within you.

a poem from my nieces and nephews before the 1996 Olympics

About the Author

At just over 5'2" tall, and not having made her first Olympic team until the age of 27, Sheila Taormina seems an unlikely candidate to have competed in four consecutive summer Olympiads in three completely different sports (Swimming 1996, Triathlon 2000 and 2004, Pentathlon 2008). Her first two attempts to qualify for the Olympics in swimming (1988 and 1992), came up short, during what were considered her "peak" years. Following those years she moved forward with her education, finishing her Masters degree in Business in 1994, and then began her professional career in the automotive industry that same year, working a full-time salaried position in Detroit.

With her eyes set on the possibilities of 1996, she trained before and after work, at her small, hometown swim team in Livonia, Michigan. There were no corporate endorsements fueling the effort - just a plan, some hard work, and a coach who believed along with her. Sheila learned about technique, efficiency, and the keys to success. Applying those throughout the years, Sheila grew to become Olympic champion in one sport, world champion in a second sport, and the world cup standings leader in a third sport.

In the end, Sheila Taormina has experienced six completely different disciplines on the Olympic stage - swimming, cycling, running, pistol shooting, fencing, and equestrian show jumping. Her perspective on the Olympics, human potential, and performance is unparalleled. Please visit www.sheilat.com for more information.

USA Olympic team members, Allison Schmitt and Sheila Taormina

Notes

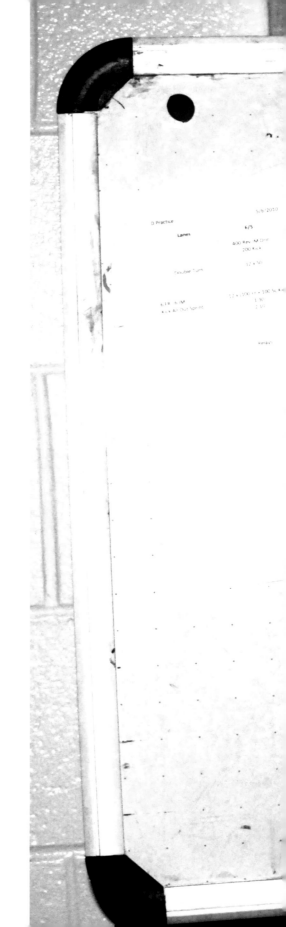

300 Rev Im
200 Kick

Never give Up!

Notes

Notes

Notes